Lustres

La Jouaillier.

N. de l'Armessin jnven. et. sculp.

a Paris Chez N. de l'Armessin Rue S. Iaques pres la Rue du Platre a la Coupe d'Or, Avec Privilege du Roy. 1608.

JEWELS AND JEWELLERY

JEWELS
AND
JEWELLERY

Clare Phillips

Photography by Ian Thomas

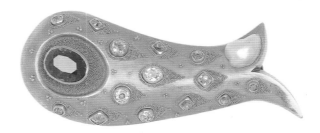

V&A Publications

In memory of Shirley Bury and Jean Schofield

First published by V&A Publications, 2000

V&A Publications
160 Brompton Road
London SW3 1HW

Photography by Ian Thomas

Designed by Bernard Higton

ISBN 1 85177 279 0

A catalogue record for this book is available from the
British Library.

Printed in Hong Kong by South Sea International Press

Jacket illustrations:
Front: Enamelled necklace, France, *c.*1660 (page 53)
Back: Necklace by Hermann Jünger, Germany, 1990. (page 135)

Endpapers: *La Jouaillier*, Bibliothèque Nationale, Paris
Frontispiece: Portrait of Lady Cory with a Dog

Contents

ACKNOWLEDGEMENTS

This book could not have been written without the
encouragement and energy of Philippa Glanville. I am
deeply grateful to her for enabling me to withdraw from
my usual duties to concentrate on it, and to Paul
Greenhalgh for providing the support of the Research
Department. Profound thanks are due to Richard
Edgcumbe, whose scholarship and generosity have made
a particular contribution. I am indebted to my husband
for not only his unfailing support but also his relentless
eye for detail.

The book has benefited from the advice of many
specialists and enthusiasts, amongst whom I must
particularly thank Lesley Coldham of De Beers, David
Beasley of the Goldsmiths' Company, Kathleen Slater of
the Crafts Council, Gilles Grandjean of the Musée des
Beaux-Arts, Rouen, Nigel Israel, Sheila Weatherby and
Michael Fay – all of whom have been exceptionally
helpful. I have drawn also on the great wealth of expertise
within the Museum and am grateful to Lucy Cullen for
her advice on cameos; Ann Eatwell and Pippa Shirley for
references and illustrations found while they were
working on the new Silver Galleries; Charles Newton for
introducing me to Mr Sponge; Anthony North for
reflections on cut steel; the late Clive Wainwright for his
many insights into the nineteenth century; and Matthew
Winterbottom for his research on jewellery made from
humming-birds and beetles. Malcolm Baker, Marian
Campbell, Katie Coombs, Louise Hofman, Dominic
Naish, Susan North, Halina Pasierbska, Angus Patterson,
Andrew Spira, Eleanor Townsend, Eric Turner and
Rowan Watson have also contributed useful references,
ideas and practical support.

Briony Hudson, Guy Turner and Annette Wickhan
supervised the photographic programme and the
measuring of pieces, and I am most grateful for their
enthusiasm and diligence. I would also like to express my
appreciation of the V&A's Metalwork Conservation
Department and particularly thank Joanna Whalley for
the many hours she devoted to cleaning pieces before they
were photographed. Mary Butler, Miranda Harrison and
Mary Wessel of V&A Publications, designer Bernard
Higton and editor Helen Armitage have seen the book
through from conception to production, and I am most
grateful to them all.

The glory of the book is the superb photography by Ian
Thomas, whose imagination and technical mastery have
brought these pieces to life.

INTRODUCTION

The Victoria & Albert Museum has one of the world's finest and most comprehensive jewellery collections. This book draws on its range and quality to illustrate the development of Western jewellery over the last 500 years. The Museum, which was named the Victoria & Albert Museum in 1899, had its origins in the 1840s in the galleries attached to the School of Design at Somerset House in London. With Prince Albert's support, proceeds from the Great Exhibition of 1851 were used to expand and relocate these collections. The result was the opening of the South Kensington Museum under Henry Cole in 1857. The Museum's aim was – and remains – to increase appreciation and enjoyment of the decorative arts amongst as broad an audience as possible. It sought particularly to improve the standard of contemporary design through promoting a wider knowledge of the past.

Since the 1850s the Museum has been acquiring beautiful, technically challenging and innovative jewellery as an important element of its displays. Many of these acquisitions have been the result of generous donations, notably those by Dame Joan Evans, Lady Cory and the Reverend Chauncey Hare Townshend. The bulk of the collection dates from medieval times through to the present day, though there are a few earlier pieces from the Bronze Age through to the Byzantine period. It is especially strong in the jewellery of the eighteenth and nineteenth centuries, and in the work of contemporary artist–jewellers. While the Museum has many important oriental pieces – especially from India – this book concentrates purely on those within the Western tradition.

The book is divided into three parts. The first section describes the materials used by jewellers: metals; gemstones; enamels and organic matter from pearls to early plastics. The second looks chronologically at the development of styles in jewellery since the Middle Ages. And the third describes aspects of how jewellery was hallmarked, distributed and used over recent centuries.

Most of the pieces illustrated are on display in the V&A's Jewellery Gallery, which contains more than 4500 objects. The book does not aim to detail the collection in its entirety nor can it give more than a representative selection from any one period. For those who seek further details, the summary catalogue of the Jewellery Gallery and books about specific aspects of the collection are listed in the bibliography.

PART I

MATERIALS

GOLD

Gold has been central to jewellery since at least the middle of the third millennium BC. Its rarity and its beauty – which is resistant to tarnish and most corrosive agents – have made it precious to all civilizations, while its softness in the natural state made it easy to work with primitive tools. The earliest sources of gold were alluvial: fine particles eroded from the rock, which were collected by panning the silt of stream and riverbeds. However, by Roman times open-cast and tunnel mining were practised in Europe. During the sixteenth and seventeenth centuries great quantities of gold were brought from the New World, imported into Europe by the Spanish. It was subsequently discovered in California in 1848, in Australia in 1851 and in South Africa in the 1880s.

Until 1975 standards of purity in gold were often measured in carats (karats in the United States of America) with pure gold – seldom used today because of its softness – being 24 carats. More commonly found is 18 carat (75 per cent pure) and 9 carat, which contains only 33 per cent pure gold. The remaining proportion may be made up from a variety of metals, which can contribute hardness and colour to the gold. In the *Encyclopédie* of 1751–65, Diderot listed five colours of gold: yellow, which was pure gold; red, which was three parts gold to one part pink copper; green, which was usually three parts gold to one part fine silver; grey or blue, caused by adding arsenic or steel filings to the gold; and white,

which he explained was really silver, sometimes with a small amount of gold added to soften its brilliancy. Over the centuries goldsmiths have experimented to create many other variants and subtleties of shade.

Gold's properties make it suitable for many techniques. One of the most intricate and ancient is Etruscan granulation, where minute grains of gold are attached without solder to a gold background, creating either a powdery surface texture or a precise pattern. During the Archaeological Revival of the mid-nineteenth century (see page 82) this technique fascinated goldsmiths. However, it was not until the twentieth century that it was found that if the grains were held in place with copper carbonate, water and fish glue, on heating the copper fuses with the gold to create an invisible, solder-less join. An innovation of the late twentieth century is the gold 'clay' developed by Mitsubishi Materials. Fine particles of gold dust are blended into a putty that is modelled then fired at a high temperature, burning off the binding agent and leaving a pure gold form.

Top: Gold bullion from the wrecked Spanish galleon *Nuestra Señora de las Maravillas*, which sank in 1656. The marks identify their purity and the foundry, in which they were processed, and show that duty had been paid.

Below: Lid of a late eighteenth-century Swiss box, the decoration made of contrasting colours of gold (length 8.6cm/3.4in). The central trophy celebrates contemporary ballooning initiatives.

Top right: One of a pair of Etruscan gold rosettes from the seventh century BC, decorated with granulation (diameter 4cm/1.6in).

Bottom right: The Shannongrove Gorget, a gold collar made in c. seventh century BC in Ireland, a country that was particularly rich in alluvial gold during the Bronze Age (diameter of discs 9.5cm/3.7in).

SILVER AND PLATINUM

Bracelet of 'oxidized' silver set with cabochon emeralds, by Parisian jeweller F. J. Rudolphi, who showed a similar bracelet, designed by Masson, at the Great Exhibition of 1851. The metal was coloured using a sulphide solution (height 6.2cm/2.4in).

In 1712 the English noblewoman Lady Pawlet was described at a wedding 'in all her finery of true lovers knots of diamonds set in as much silver as would make a pair of candle-sticks'. Throughout the eighteenth and nineteenth centuries diamonds were set in silver rather than gold, as the whiteness of the metal was felt better to complement the brilliance of the stones. Although the description of Lady Pawlet is exaggerated for effect, settings then were much bulkier than those of today. Silver's softness prompted jewellers to encase stones with it around the sides and underneath, and the weight of metal used would be incorporated in the cost of the finished jewel. Although silver is found throughout Europe, most of it in use at this date was imported from Mexico, Peru, Chile and Bolivia. In about 1800 more delicate open-backed settings were introduced, with a ring of silver holding the stone around its widest point or girdle. The later nineteenth century saw a dramatic increase in the production of jewellery made entirely of silver due to the discovery in 1860 of the extensive Comstock Lode of silver in West Nevada in the United States of America. Much of this was cheaper mass-produced work.

To clean the tarnish from silver-set jewellery *Queen* magazine of July 1880 offered various recipes that included the use of spirit of ammonium, lemon juice and arrowroot. Alternatively, it suggested the 'Maltese' method of boiling in soapy water, scrubbing gently while hot, rinsing and then drying on a piece of unglazed earthenware heated in the fire. This latter detail made 'every particle of moisture to evaporate, which otherwise would remain on the silver and cause it to tarnish or assume a greenish hue'.

Platinum, first found in South America, was named *plata* by the Spanish settlers – a derivation of their word for silver. Although strong and with an untarnishing lustre, it was for many years used only seldom in jewellery, due to its rarity and the very high temperature required to melt it. One of the earliest English references to its use is the record of the Prince of Wales' purchase of a 'platina' watch chain in 1805. Its modern role for setting diamonds dates back to about 1870, although it was not until around 1900 that its use became widespread. It was particularly fashionable in the 1920s and 1930s when strong unobtrusive settings were required to show off dense concentrations of diamonds.

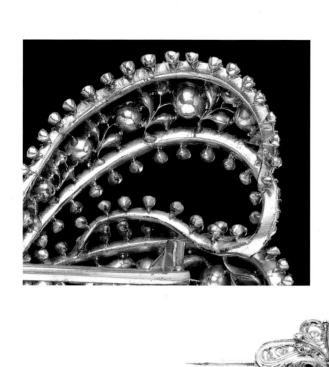

The enclosed backs, typical of eighteenth-century silver settings, can be seen in this detail of the back of a Russian diamond-bow ornament, c.1760 (the front is illustrated on page 61).

Silver filigree brooch, probably made in Germany in the eighteenth century (height 3.4cm/1.3in). Filigree is a simple technique that capitalizes on the malleability of wire. It has been used for centuries across Europe, and pieces can therefore be very difficult to date.

Untarnishing settings of delicacy and strength were possible with platinum, as in this diamond and onyx brooch made by Cartier, Paris, c.1912, and sold in their New York branch at Christmas 1913 (length 5.1cm/2in).

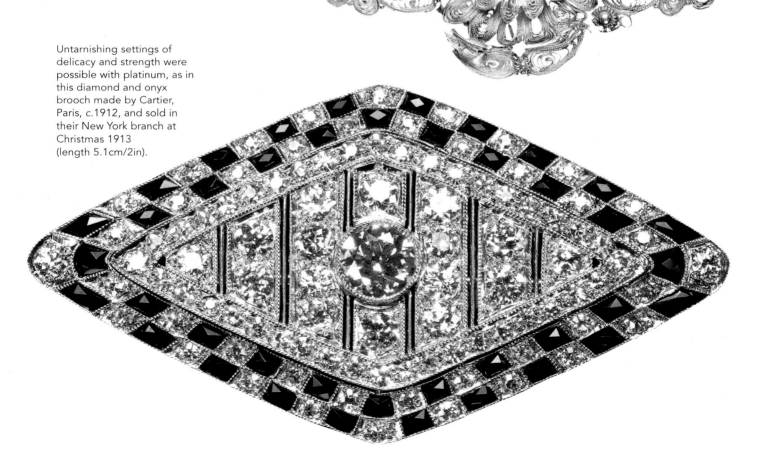

BASE METALS

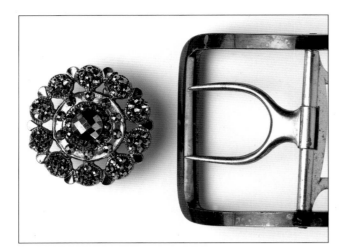

Although less highly prized, base metals have remained in constant use in jewellery from a very early date. Some of the most plentiful survivals are rings, and the V&A's collection includes Etruscan bronze rings from around 400 BC, Roman examples in iron, bronze and lead, Anglo-Saxon ones of twisted wire and medieval bronze signet rings. Large iron buckles inlaid with elaborate geometric patterns in silver were made by the Merovingians between the fifth and the eighth century. Their corroded surfaces prove the lasting supremacy of gold and indicate why so few iron pieces have survived.

Base metals were frequently plated with silver or gold to give the appearance of precious metal. Alloys that resembled gold were invented, most famously pinchbeck, a mixture of copper and zinc invented by the London watchmaker Christopher Pinchbeck some time before 1732. Jewellery made of cut steel became fashionable in the late eighteenth century and remained popular for the next hundred years. The metallic glitter of its faceted-steel surface (see page 64) created a similar effect to that of marcasite, the yellow-grey crystals of iron pyrites, which were set in jewellery around the same time. In the early nineteenth century black-iron jewellery of incredible delicacy was produced in Germany (see page 72). Although made from a humble metal, these pieces were highly valued and were sometimes mounted in gold.

Aluminium enjoyed great celebrity when a process for refining it was first discovered in the 1850s. Regarded briefly as a precious metal it was used alongside gold until the early 1860s, when improved technology enabled easier and cheaper production, resulting in its sudden loss of value. Its descent was dramatic: the first kilogram refined in 1854 had been priced at 3000 francs, after five years this dropped to 400 francs, and by 1899 the price had further fallen to a mere 3.5 francs per kilogram. In recent years aluminium has been revived and transformed by metalworkers such as British jeweller Jane Adam – who paints and anodizes the surface to create a myriad of different colours. Similar vivid surfaces have been achieved by craftsmen working with the refractory metals, titanium and niobium, while the greyer beauties of steel and iron have been explored by modern jewellers seeking materials that express alternative values to those of the costly precious metals.

Top left: Decorative treatments of steel: a cut-steel button and a detail of a steel buckle blued by heat or acid, both English, *c*.1800 (diameter of button 2.6cm/1in).

Below: Bracelet of aluminium and gilt metal, made in France, *c*.1870 (length 18.8cm/7.4in). Aluminium is resistant to soldering, so the engraved panels have been rivetted on to the gilt metal frame.

Niobium earrings made by British jeweller Alan Craxford, 1984 (length 10.2cm/4in). The shimmering colours were created by submerging the piece in an anodic bath and passing controlled electric currents through it.

Section of a marcasite and blue-glass necklace with silvered copper settings, probably French from the early nineteenth century. Marcasite resembles cut steel but differs in the delicacy of its setting – usually a conventional jeweller's setting as opposed to the more basic rivets of cut steel.

Ring of tin inlaid with gold, made by Austrian jeweller Fritz Maierhofer, 1980.

DIAMONDS

Left: An eighteenth-century Dutch diamond-grading box (diameter 15cm/6in) made of brass, with 44 sieve plates that vary in fineness from the size of a pinhole to a 3-carat stone. John Mawe in 1823 explained that 'for the purpose of more easily separating the greater stones from the smaller, the merchant has small sieves or boxes of tin, with numerous holes punched in them'. The cylindrical box opens in the middle for the appropriate sieve and then the stones to be inserted. When not in use the sieve plates are stored within the box.

Diamonds deserve the chief regard of all jewels. First, They are the best repository of wealth; inasmuch as they will lie in the smallest space of any, and are thereby the most portable, and best conveyance of treasure. Next, their superlative Hardness secures them from all injury by wear; as nothing can make any impression on them, or prejudice their lustre, but their rubbing against each other.

DAVID JEFFRIES, *A TREATISE ON DIAMONDS AND PEARLS* (1750)

Named from the Greek *adamas*, meaning invincible, diamonds were known in Europe from Roman times. They were treasured initially for their hardness and their perceived magical qualities, and in the Middle Ages enjoyed a fearful reputation, powdered, as a poison. However, only small quantities reached Europe until the Renaissance. By the early sixteenth century the development of diamond points and table-cuts allowed the brilliance of the stone to be appreciated. These were set in gold enclosed to just above the widest point, or girdle, and gave quite a dark glitter. From the 1620s the rose cut was used in Europe, with a flat base beneath a dome of triangular facets. Greater sparkle was achieved through the brilliant cut with its 58 facets, which first appeared in the late seventeenth century. With slight modifications this remains the most typical cut to this day.

India was the source of diamonds throughout the earlier centuries, and its mines were described by the seventeenth-century French traveller and gem dealer

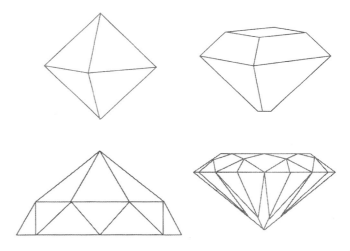

Above, clockwise from top left: Diagram of different cuts: octahedral crystal, table cut, brilliant cut, rose cut.

Jean-Baptiste Tavernier. The Indian deposits were close to exhaustion when diamonds were discovered in Brazil in 1725, and, similarly, almost a century and a half later, the Brazilian mines were largely finished when diamonds were found in South Africa in 1866. During the twentieth century further sources have been located in other parts of Africa as well as Russia, Australia and Canada.

Left: Diamonds of different colours, set as rings (*from the top*): an unpolished octahedron crystal; a brilliant-cut white; yellow – found mostly in South Africa, the colour caused by nitrogen; green – caused by prolonged exposure to natural radiation but very rare for it to penetrate evenly throughout the stone; dark green; blue – found infrequently in India and caused by boron; pink – found in minute quantities in India, Brazil and Tanzania, and now in greater abundance in NW Australia; and black – caused by extensive graphite inclusions, normally only used industrially.

Right: Design for a pendant by Arnold Lulls from the early seventeenth century. The diamonds are shown black, just as they are in paintings of the period – an indication of the darker glitter of the table-cut stone.

COLOURED GEMSTONES: THE TOWNSHEND COLLECTION

Neither silks, nor paints, nor even enamels can ever equal the colours of precious stones in durability, or in brilliancy and pulsating variety of hue.

So wrote A. H. Church in 1883 in *Precious Stones*, the catalogue of gems from the Townshend Collection. This important collection of 145 gems had been bequeathed to the South Kensington Museum, as the V&A was then known, in 1869 and was to be further augmented by Church's own collection in 1913. Although it does not compete with the comprehensive nature of the Natural History Museum's collections, it is of particular historical interest as its formation pre-dates the development of many artificial enhancements and synthetic gemstones.

The nineteenth-century curator G. F. Duncombe recounted how this generous bequest had come to the V&A: 'Some years ago the Rev. Chauncy Hare Townshend … while walking with me through the Museum stopped to examine the jewels exhibited in the South Court, and to compare them with those in his own collection. Mr Townshend having no children, it occurred to me that it would be a noble thing for him to leave his collection by will to the South Kensington Museum, which at that time had no precious stones except on loan. I made the suggestion to him, and he seemed pleased with the idea, and subsequently often referred to it … I have since had the satisfaction of learning that about three years ago, Mr Townshend added a codicil to his will, by which he more than carried out the suggestion that I ventured originally to him'.

It was a major acquisition for the museum and generated great interest. In April 1870 the ladies' magazine *London Society* used the museum in the plot of 'A Romance of South Kensington', mentioning what is almost certainly the Townshend Collection: 'Some cases of coins and gems had recently been deposited here by one of those enlightened public benefactors who from time to time yield up the contents of their galleries and cabinets for the benefit of the British public. Just then a young lady, attended by her maid, passed on to the cabinet of gems …With an eager curiosity she examined specimens; in a dainty little memorandum, in true artist fashion, she made a slight sketch or two'. Twenty years later they almost certainly inspired Oscar Wilde, who for his vivid description of Dorian's collection of jewels in *The Picture of Dorian Gray* borrowed significantly from Church's descriptions in *Precious Stones*.

In order to be used successfully in jewellery, coloured gemstones must combine beauty with an adequate level of hardness. Amongst the most highly prized of coloured gemstones are the emerald, the ruby and the blue sapphire (ruby and blue sapphire are both varieties of corundum). Unlike diamonds these stones were used in jewellery at an early date as their colour remained attractive even before faceting was possible. In Late Roman jewellery – where diamonds are virtually unknown – natural hexagonal emerald crystals from Egypt were threaded on gold wire alongside irregular polished sapphires probably brought from Sri Lanka. During the Middle Ages red spinels, known as balas rubies, enjoyed equal prestige to the pink Sri Lankan rubies – and the magnificent Black Prince's Ruby in the English Crown Jewels is in fact a spinel. By the time of the Renaissance the deep rubies and sapphires from Burma were known, and dark Colombian emeralds became available in Europe following Columbus's voyage of 1492. With the exception of the Egyptian emerald mines, which gave out centuries ago, these early sources remain important producers of coloured gemstones, augmented by discoveries of other gem deposits throughout the world.

In addition to these well-known stones, jewellers are able to draw on a host of others to achieve a wide range of subtle shades. The early nineteenth century witnessed a burst of multicoloured jewellery with topazes, aquamarines and chrysoberyls from Brazil and Siberian amethysts. In modern times there is a popular tradition of birthstones, where particular gems are linked to months of the year and are believed to bring luck to those whose birthdays they represent. Selections vary, but January is usually associated with garnet, February amethyst, March aquamarine, April diamond, May emerald, June pearl, July ruby, August peridot, September sapphire, October opal, November topaz and December turquoise. This superstitious aspect to gemstones is a shadowy reminder of medieval lapidary, when gemstones were believed to bestow particular blessings and healing on the wearer.

Rings set with coloured stones (*from left to right*):
(row 1) Emerald, Ruby, Sapphire, Sapphire, Sapphire, Sapphire;
(row 2) Spinel, Citrine, Amethyst, Aquamarine, Peridot, Chrysoberyl;
(row 3) Tourmaline, Tourmaline, Zircon, Zircon, Topaz, Topaz;
(row 4) Garnet, Demantoid Garnet, Hessonite Garnet, Opal, Black Opal, Fire Opal;
(row 5) Chrysoberyl Cat's Eye, Star Sapphire, Star Ruby, Moonstone, Labradorite;
(row 6) Chrysoprase, Turquoise, Malachite, Lapis Lazuli, Chalcedony, Aventurine Quartz;
(row 7) Onyx, Moss Agate, Cornelian, Agate, Jasper.

PEARLS

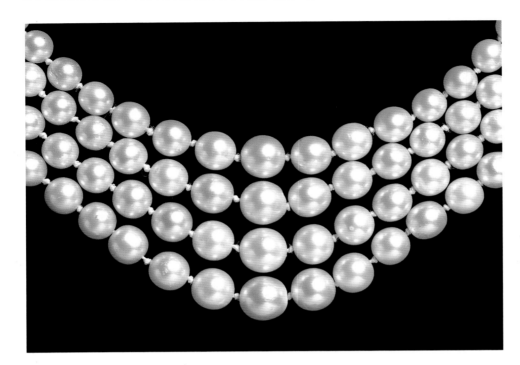

Cultured pearls strung in graduated rows, detail of a necklace that was probably made in England between 1900 and 1910 (diameter of largest pearl 0.8cm/0.3in).

Those of the finest shape are perfectly round, which fits them for necklaces, bracelets, jewels for the hair, and other such like uses. But if a Pearl, of any considerable size, be of the shape of a Pear, it is not reckoned an imperfection, because it may be suitable for drops to earrings, solitairs [sic], and many other jewels. Their complexion must be milk white, not of a dead and lifeless, but of a clear and lively hue, free from stains, fouls, spots, specks, or roughness; such are of the highest esteem and value.
DAVID JEFFRIES, *A TREATISE ON DIAMONDS AND PEARLS* (1750)

For centuries necklaces of well-matched round pearls have been amongst the most prestigious of jewels. Their preferred length has varied according to fashion, from the long ropes worn by Queen Elizabeth and her courtiers, which fell below the waist, to the neat strings encircling the necks of Restoration beauties and the close-fitting rows of Edwardian dog-collars.

Pearls are formed when an irritant such as a particle of grit enters the shell of a mollusc and gradually becomes coated with layers of iridescent nacre. From the Middle Ages they have been imported into Europe from the Persian Gulf and the Gulf of Mannar, the part of the Indian Ocean between SE India and Sri Lanka. Over the centuries further sources have been found, including the waters around Venezuela, the Pacific Islands and Western Australia. A pearl's porosity makes it sensitive to humidity and acidic materials, and to keep its lustre requires some care: in October 1871 *Queen* magazine advised: 'Wear your pearls as often as possible. When not worn, keep them wrapped in blue paper. Once a year they should be re-strung and washed with a lather of soap and water; but your jeweller should send a woman to do that – do not attempt it yourself.'

Freshwater pearls, known in the Middle Ages as Scotch pearls due to their being found in (amongst other places) Scottish rivers, have long provided a cheaper but less lustrous alternative. In addition man-made imitations have been available from an early date: Bolognese pearl recipes of the fifteenth century combined ground mother-of-pearl with gum arabic and dew, or mixed snail slime with egg white. Imitation pearls have remained popular items of costume jewellery: Loelia, Duchess of Westminster, noted the 1924 fashion for 'choker pearls, the size of gooseberries' and commented that 'up till then it had been thought good taste to wear small Tècla pearls, of a size in proportion to one's income, so that they might be mistaken for real'. However, the most effective competition, which was to have a devastating effect on the price of natural pearls, came with the development of cultured ones. This process, where irritants are systematically inserted into farmed oysters, was pioneered by Kokichi Mikimoto of Japan in the early twentieth century. A regular shape can be guaranteed, and although the nacre may only be a thin coating, it has the natural lustre of a real pearl.

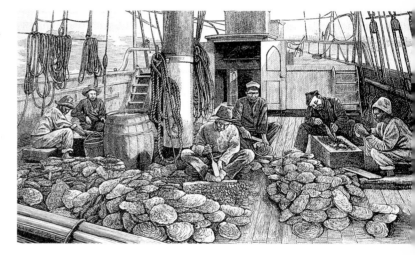

Top: Seed-pearl necklace made in England, c.1820. These minute pearls are pierced and threaded on silk or horsehair to form lacelike patterns, the larger elements are attached to mother-of-pearl frames (maximum width 4cm/1.6in).

Left: Baroque or irregular pearls were ingeniously used in Renaissance jewellery. This merman, with its pearl torso, is known as the Canning Jewel after the 2nd Viscount Canning, who acquired it in India, c.1860. Originally believed to date from the sixteenth century, it is now thought more likely to be a Renaissance revival jewel of the nineteenth century (height 10.2cm/4in).

Above: Checking oyster shells for pearls on board *Sree Pas-Sair*, the schooner sent by London jeweller Edwin Streeter in the early 1880s to search for pearls off Western Australia.

OTHER ORGANIC MATERIALS

Materials from animals and plants – such as animal teeth, feathers, shells, flowers and berries – were used in jewellery long before man was able to employ tools to fashion metal or stone. Living organisms have continued to contribute colour and variety to the wealth of substances provided by the natural world.

Two nineteenth-century star brooches made of tortoiseshell decorated with piqué or gold and silver inlay (height 4cm/1.6in). Tortoiseshell, usually from the hawksbill and caret turtles, was softened in boiling salted water before being moulded in heated dies. The pattern was engraved into the surface, then filled with tiny flakes of precious metal. Piqué was traditionally a French and Italian speciality, although by the early 1870s it was also produced in Birmingham.

Above: Carved ivory scene, framed with zircons and set in the bezel of an eighteenth-century gold ring. Ivory was imported from India, Sri Lanka and Africa, and its carving was principally a Continental speciality – several towns in Southern Germany were known for it, including Erbach, where a school and workshop was established in 1781, and there were also centres in Switzerland and France. Today elephants are a protected species, and the sale of ivory is restricted by international law.

Right: Brooch of bog-oak in silver-gilt mounts, with moulded Celtic decoration, made in Ireland, c.1860 (height 7cm/2.8in). This material, basically wood that has been hardened and blackened by long immersion in a peat bog, is particular to Ireland. As a result, nationalistic shamrocks, harps and round towers are typical decorations. In 1852 mechanical stamping of bog-oak was introduced, enabling more complex patterns but less sharp delineation than had been possible with hand-carving.

Detail of a tiara made from polished branches of coral, made in Italy, c.1830–50. Coral is formed from the skeletons of tiny marine polyps, and most of that used in Victorian jewellery was from the seas around Italy, where it was fished between April and July. *The Illustrated London News* commented in 1851 that: 'The price varies from 1s. per oz up to £5 and £20 per oz. The best colours are considered a bright red or pale pink.' Various imitations were available in the late nineteenth century, including early plastics, stained ivory and French coraline made of coloured alabaster.

Right: Bracelet band of plaited and twisted human hair, the gold clasp set with a shell cameo, probably made in Switzerland, c.1825 (length 20.3cm/8in). Hair is often found in sentimental jewellery, either a hidden curl within a locket or more publicly displayed on the bezel of a mourning ring. For much of the nineteenth century hair was fashionable for more general use – either woven by professional hair-workers or by amateurs at home following the instructions in books such as Mrs Speight's *The Lock of Hair* (1871). Cameos were particularly fashionable in the early nineteenth century, and those of shell (usually conch shells from as far afield as Jamaica or Madagascar) were quicker and cheaper to carve than those of hardstone. Classical themes were popular; this one is thought perhaps to represent Alexander, Roxana and a genius with torch and arrow.

Amber-coloured belt buckle of celluloid made between 1920 and 1930 (diameter 6.2cm/2.4in.). Derived from plant cells rather than taken directly from nature, celluloid – a cellulose-nitrate compound – was developed, c.1870, by the American brothers James and Isaiah Hyatt. It was not the first plastic – which was Parkesine, patented by Alexander Parkes of Birmingham in 1855 – but it was one of the ones used most extensively for jewellery.

Brooch of ostrich-egg inlay on wood, set in bronze, designed and made by American jeweller Thomas Gentille, 1982 (diameter 7.6cm/3in). Eggshell was also used in the 1920s, principally for accessories, where it provided crazed white geometric blocks.

GLASS AND ENAMEL

Glass has featured in jewellery since man first understood how it is made. Glass beads have been excavated widely, with finds dating back to the third millennium BC in Mesopotamia and the Caucasus. Its other persistent role in jewellery, that of imitating precious stones, was established by the Egyptians in at least 1500 BC.

Recipes for different coloured-glass stones survive from the Middle Ages, when they were used both for ecclesiastical purposes – for decorating reliquaries and book-covers – and for secular pieces such as children's jewellery and funerary ornaments. The Venetian island of Murano was the principal centre for their production. The city authorities had mixed feelings about this speciality: anxious for it not to interfere with the trade in real gems they imposed heavy penalties for any deliberate deceptions, while at the same time they were keen to prevent the craftsmen from emigrating and establishing rival centres. However, glassmakers did leave, and flourishing industries developed elsewhere in Europe, notably in Bohemia and France. These countries were particularly important producers during the eighteenth century, which was an especially splendid period for paste or imitation jewellery.

Enamel has very similar properties to glass and is made from the same basic ingredients: ground flint or sand, red lead, soda or potash, and a metallic oxide colouring agent – copper for green, cobalt for blue, iron for red and brown, manganese for purple. These are heated together to form blocks of different coloured glass. They are then ground to a fine powder, washed and mixed with water to form the paste that, when fired, becomes enamel. Enamel may be applied to gold, silver and copper. The surface of the metal must usually be roughened or engraved to help the enamel to adhere, and successive layers and firings are required to produce an even and deep colour. With translucent enamel the need for a roughened surface may be put to decorative effect, as in medieval figurative scenes and in the precise engine-turned patterns visible beneath the enamel of eighteenth-century boxes. Different enamelling techniques give very different effects: in cloisonné enamel the design is made up of a series of metal cells, each of which contains one colour; in *plique à jour* the cells are unbacked, creating an effect like stained glass; in *champlevé*, the design is engraved into the metal, leaving depressions that are then filled with one or more colours. The enamelling of three-dimensional forms, introduced at the end of the Middle Ages, was known as *émail en ronde-bosse* or encrusted enamel. Further subtlety may be achieved by painting different coloured enamels on to the metal.

Plaque of *émail en resille* on brown glass, mounted in silver gilt (length 3.8cm/1.5in). An intricate technique thought to have originated in France in the late sixteenth century: the design is engraved into the glass panel, the hollows lined with gold leaf then filled with different colours of enamel and fired.

Above: Pendant with elements of glass fused to ceramic, on a silver circlet. Designed and made by self-taught American jeweller Elsa Freund, 1965 (height of pendant 6.9cm/2.7in).

Below: *Pâte-de-verre* pendant on a tasselled cord by French designer Gabriel Argy-Rousseau, *c.*1921 (diameter 6.3cm/2.5in). This unusual material is made from a paste of ground glass of different colours, which is sculpted or moulded, fired and then cooled very slowly.

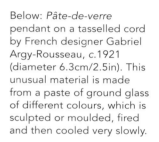

Enamelled gold ring set with a star of point-cut pastes, European, made in the early seventeenth century. The worn edges of the pastes are a crude indication that they are not diamonds.

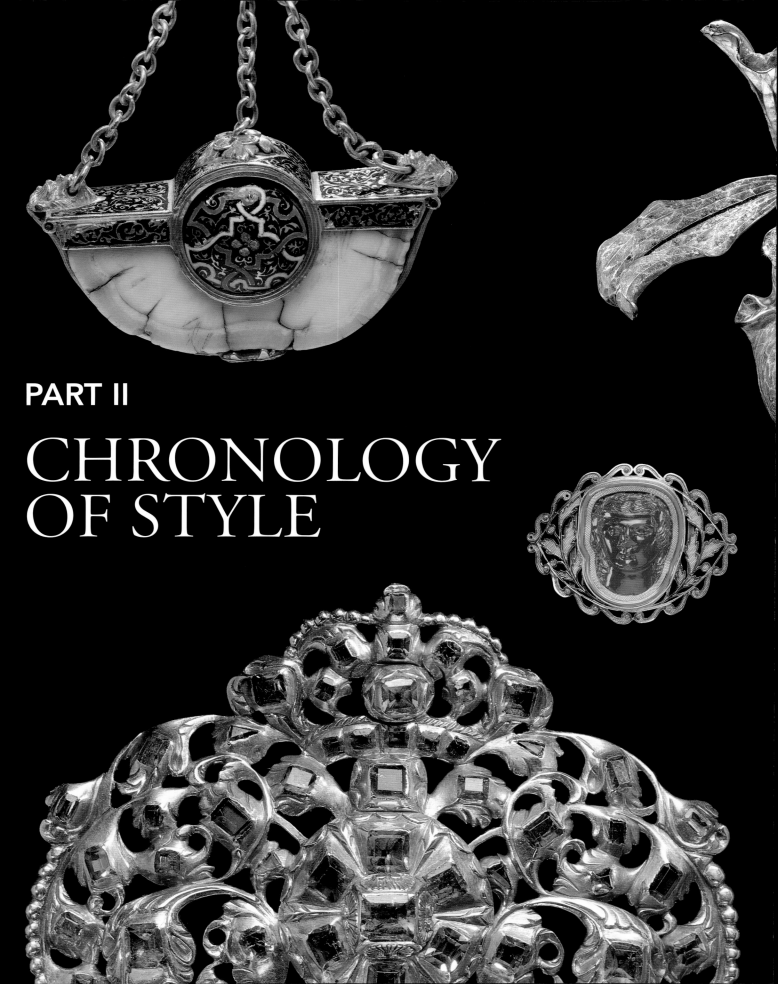

PART II
CHRONOLOGY OF STYLE

MASTERPIECES OF THE MIDDLE AGES

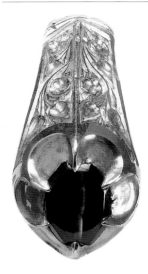

Gold and sapphire ring, which belonged to William Wytlesey, Archbishop of Canterbury between 1362 and 1374. His name is inscribed inside, and the ring is said to have been found in his tomb.

Jewellery was worn by men, women and children throughout the Middle Ages. Many pieces, such as girdles and ring brooches, had a functional role in dress. Some had heraldic significance and many more a devotional aspect. The two dominant themes in European jewellery at this time were religion and courtly love. This is most obvious in figurative designs, but it is equally true of the decorative inscriptions so often found on rings and ring brooches. One might carry the opening words of the prayer to the Virgin Mary '*Ave Maria gracia plena dom*', while another '*Ami amet deli pencet*', which translates as 'Think of a friend who loves you'. In many jewels the devotional and the worldly were closely intertwined, and this was perhaps most marked in the luxuriant paternosters and rosaries, on which people counted their prayers and which were so proudly displayed in portraits.

Gold and silver were the preferred metals for jewellery, decorated with enamels, niello (a black alloy of silver, sulphur and lead) and gemstones – notably sapphires, rubies and pearls. Until the later Middle Ages gems were polished rather than faceted, giving pebble-like shapes and soft pools of colour. Stones were chosen not just for colour but also for their supposed healing and spiritual powers, which were extensively written about and widely accepted. According to the treatise on lapidary written by Marbodus, an eleventh-century Bishop of Rennes, the sapphire's virtues included not only protection against physical injury, fraud, fear and envy but also the promotion of peace and reconciliation, healing for ulcers, eyes and headaches and the safeguarding of chastity. If the stone were drilled or pierced, as in William Wytlesey's ring, its effectiveness was believed to increase. Other stones had different powers, and the teeth of fossilized fish, known as toad-stones, were worn to cure dropsy and spleen.

Amongst the greatest masterpieces of medieval goldsmiths' work are the jewel-like enamel plaques, often decorated with elaborate figurative scenes. The design was first engraved into the surface of the silver or gold, then different colours of translucent enamel were applied. By varying the depth of the engraving, and thereby the thickness of the enamel, subtle effects of shading and modelling were possible. Most enamels were of religious subjects – principally scenes from the New Testament or from lives of the saints, although secular pieces are also known. They were used in portable diptychs and triptychs, pendants and girdle-ends.

By the second half of the thirteenth century increased levels of affluence in Europe had resulted in a demand for jewellery beyond court circles. Consequently, sumptuary laws were introduced to prevent the wearing of jewellery at what were considered inappropriate levels of society. In England in 1363 Edward III forbade the families of artisans and yeomen to wear 'belts, collars, clasps, rings, garters, brooches, ribbons, chains, bands or seals, or any other thing whatsoever of gold or silver', but such restrictions were seldom successful.

Case for a small book or relic (height 5.6cm/2.2in). The enamelled scene shows a knight giving his spear to a lady leaning from castle battlements, probably a scene from the *Romance of Sir Enyas and the Wodewose* (wildman). Made in England or France in the mid-1300s.

The Langdale Rosary, consisting of fifty oval 'ave' beads, six lozenge-shaped 'paternoster' beads and a single pendant (height of pendant 2.8cm/1.1in). The hollow beads are engraved and enamelled in black on each side with a saint or a scene from the life of Christ, with an explanatory inscription around each rim. The only surviving English gold rosary of the late fifteenth century, it is thought to have once belonged to Lord William Howard (1563–1640), third son of Thomas, Duke of Norfolk, and to pass by a later marriage to the Langdales, an old Yorkshire Catholic family.

Gold ring brooch decorated with rubies and sapphires in tall collets encircled with foliage, French, thirteenth century (diameter 5.4cm/2.1in).

Heart-shaped gold brooch, probably French from the fifteenth century (height 3.9cm/1.5in). The back is engraved with flowers and the black letter inscription *Nostre et tout ditz a vostre [d]eseir*, which translates as 'Ours and always at your desire'.

THE RENAISSANCE PENDANT

Left: Pendant of a ship, the carved rock-crystal hull set in enamelled gold. Probably French, c.1600 (height 6.1cm/2.4in).

Opposite: The Danny Jewel. Narwhal horn mounted in enamelled gold as a pendant, made in England c.1550 (height 8.4cm/3.3in). Formerly belonging to the Campions of Danny, Sussex.

Pendants were one of the most popular types of jewel during the Renaissance, and, except for rings, they have survived in the greatest numbers. Contemporary portraits show the immense variety of designs. Men and children usually hung them from a chain around their neck. A woman might wear them on her carcanet or necklace, from her girdle or attached to her bodice, sleeve or ruff – either pinned or tied in place with a coloured ribbon.

Because the pendants were intended to hang freely, the backs are always richly decorated, and in many cases the theme continues all the way round in the manner of a small three-dimensional sculpture. Gold and enamel were the most important materials but often alongside a wealth of gems and precious substances from diamonds to ambergris. Irregular 'baroque' pearls became very popular in the last quarter of the sixteenth century, with ingenious forms of hippocamps and salamanders built up in gold around them. Medieval beliefs in the magical properties of stones continued into the Renaissance, and for this reason gems were sometimes set in a way that allowed direct

contact with the skin, as with the open-backed settings of the prophylactic pendant overleaf. The horn of the dolphin-like narwhal, known then as unicorn horn, was valued as a detector of poison, and semi-circular sections of it were mounted on gold chains.

Many pendants reflected the whims and passions of the wearer, as well as the expanding world of the sixteenth century. From the beginning of the sixteenth century the excitement of maritime exploration and trade with distant continents was expressed in jewels shaped as galleons, sea monsters, mermaids and mermen. Queen Elizabeth's liking of animal jewels was indulged by her courtiers, whose New Year's gifts to her included a white hind, a greyhound, a scorpion, a turtledove, a nightingale and a dolphin. Particular animals might be chosen with a personal joke or reference in mind, or for a more generally understood symbolism – as in the case of the salamander, an animal believed to thrive in fire and therefore to express passionate love. Cupid was a very popular figure for pendants, while marriages might be commemorated with jewels that combined the initials of a husband and wife. Some pendants united the decorative with the functional. A multi-purpose jewel listed in the Secret Jewel House at the Tower of London in 1550 combined 'A Unicornes horne closed in golde with a Whistell and instrumentes for teth and Eares and a Diall in the toppe all golde'.

During the later sixteenth century, pendants became more symmetrical with scrolling openwork containing a central figure such as Cupid, Hercules or Charity. The layers of openwork and the figures were cast separately and then screwed in place, an economical and versatile method of production that allowed further variations during assembly. This style originated in South Germany but spread quickly throughout Europe thanks to the new printing technology that allowed the large-scale reproduction of engraved designs.

Far left: Pendant of a salamander, its body a baroque pearl set in enamelled gold and hung with a pearl drop and an emerald. Made in Europe in the late sixteenth century (height 7.1cm/2.8in).

Centre: Prophylactic pendant of gold set with a peridot and a hessonite garnet, hung with a sapphire drop and with faint traces of enamel decoration (height 5.9cm/2.3in). The settings of the stones are open at the back, and around them is inscribed *ANNANISAPTA+DEI*, a charm thought to ward off epilepsy, and *DETRAGRAMMATA IHS MARIA*, an invocation to God, Jesus and Mary. Made in England, *c.*1540–60.

Right: Pendant of Cupid in an enamelled gold frame set with rubies and hung with pearls. Made in South Germany, *c.*1600 (height 8cm/3.1in).

ECHOES OF ANTIQUITY

TANDEM SI

Renaissance jewellery was greatly affected by the revival of interest in the arts of ancient Greece and Rome. Motifs such as pediments and pillars were taken from architecture, while historical figures and classical mythology provided a major source for figurative designs. Hercules, Cupid, Leda and the Swan, and Apollo and Daphne now became popular alternatives to biblical subjects, while complete battle scenes were also taken from ancient sources and worked in miniature. Many of these designs were embossed in gold, and the great Italian goldsmith Benvenuto Cellini described how this required gold sheet (ideally of 22.5 carats) that was thicker in the middle, to allow the relief to be embossed from behind using fine steel punches.

The engraved gems carved by Greek and Roman craftsmen had been highly prized throughout the Middle Ages, augmented by Byzantine examples, which occasionally found their way to the West. However, during the Renaissance these intricate sculptures, which united the natural beauty of the mineral with supreme craftsmanship, reached new levels of prestige. Cameos,

where the design is carved in relief, were the most popular, although the more subtle intaglios, where the design is cut into the surface, made fine seals. The limited availability of ancient examples resulted in the re-establishment of gem-engraving as one of the most highly regarded of European art forms, and both ancient and contemporary examples were avidly collected by European nobility. Whether mounted on vessels, furniture or jewellery, or displayed unmounted in specially designed cabinets, they became an essential element of royal treasure chambers. In Italy in the late fifteenth century Lorenzo de' Medici and Isabella d'Este amassed renowned collections, while Cardinal Francesco Gonzaga's inventory of 1483 lists 500 gems, intaglios and cameos.

Italy became the principal centre for cameo-carving in the sixteenth century, exporting work as far as Madrid, London, Vienna and Prague. In 1515 the French king, Francis I, persuaded gem-cutter Matteo del Nassaro to move to France, and this lead to sophisticated gem-engraving in Paris. Later in the century Holy Roman Emperor Rudolph II attracted craftsmen to his court in Prague, notably Ottavio Miseroni, who worked there from 1588 to his death in 1624. Little is known of other workshops in Europe, although they undoubtedly existed in England and the Netherlands, probably drawing on a combination of Italian and local craftsmen. Multi-layered onyx and sardonyx were the most popular stones, giving contrasting shades of glossy browns and white. However, a wide range of materials were used, including gemstones and shell. Portrait heads were especially popular, some copying ancient models and others depicting contemporary figures. Cameos of Moors exerted an exotic appeal and also made good use of the natural striations of the onyx (see the Drake Jewel on page 41). Surviving cameo portraits of contemporary European rulers include Elizabeth I, Charles V and Rudolph II. Sets combining ancient and modern emperors were made, and Henri IV, King of France, is known to have had such a series mounted as buttons for his coat.

Opposite, top: Portrait of Sir Christopher Hatton, *c.*1589. He wears a cameo portrait of Queen Elizabeth on long chains around his neck, while a second cameo is displayed in his hat.

Opposite, below right: Gold hat badge embossed with the bust of a Roman emperor, English or Italian, *c.*1530–40 (diameter 4.7cm/1.9in).

Above: Ring of enamelled gold set with an onyx cameo of Medusa. The elaborate and colourful setting is typical of South German work *c.*1580.

Right: The Gatacre Jewel. The amethyst cameo of Medusa is probably late Roman, and the enamelled gold frame is thought to be English, *c.*1550–60. It formerly belonged to the Gatacre family of Shropshire and was known as the 'Fair Maid of Gatacre' (height 6.9cm/2.7in).

STATEMENTS OF FAITH

The Renaissance enjoyed a much greater diversity of subjects in jewellery than had been the case during the Middle Ages, but, within this variety, Christian imagery remained extremely strong and devotional pieces continued in widespread use. As well as biblical scenes and illustrations from Saints' Lives, a wealth of internationally recognized symbols were used to represent the Deity and Christian virtues. Whilst the Reformation resulted in the suppression of some types of jewels in Protestant areas of Europe and the promotion of others in Catholic countries, universal symbols like the Cross remained in constant use across the Continent.

The sixteenth-century fashion for sculptural animal pendants found religious expression in the creation of enamelled gold pelicans and sheep. The fable of the pelican drawing blood from its own breast to feed its young had, since the Middle Ages, been used as an allegory for Christ's sacrifice, known as the pelican in its piety, as was the symbol of the Lamb of God. Similarly secular jewelled monograms had their religious counterparts. The sacred monogram IHS, which was derived from the Greek word for Jesus, maintained its popularity throughout Europe from the fifteenth to the seventeenth century. IHS jewels occur frequently on portraits, and several have survived to show how well the rectangular hog-back diamonds fit the angular gothic letters. Less widespread was the (usually Spanish) monogram of the Virgin Mary, in which the letters MARIA were combined.

In England the Reformation resulted in the banning of what were considered particularly Catholic items, or 'vaine and superstitious Thynges from the Bysshop or Sea of Rome' in 1571. These included paternosters and rosaries, reliquaries linked to the Virgin Mary or a saint, fragments of the True Cross and *Agnus Dei* medallions. These latter were made of wax from the Easter candles, stamped with the image of the Lamb of God and blessed by the Pope. Recusant catholic use of the rosary ring rather than rosary beads increased as a more discreet way to count one's prayers – these rings had ten ridges around the hoop, on which to count the ten 'aves' that made up each decade or section of the rosary.

The most dramatic religious pieces were the *memento mori* jewels, with their unflinching display of the symbols of death and their underlying message 'remember you must die'. Their intention was to encourage virtuous living, rather in the spirit of *vanitas* paintings, by reminding the wearer that they would have to account for their sins on the Day of Judgement. Rings decorated with enamelled skulls were the most frequently occurring types, but more elaborate pendants were also worn during the sixteenth and early seventeenth century.

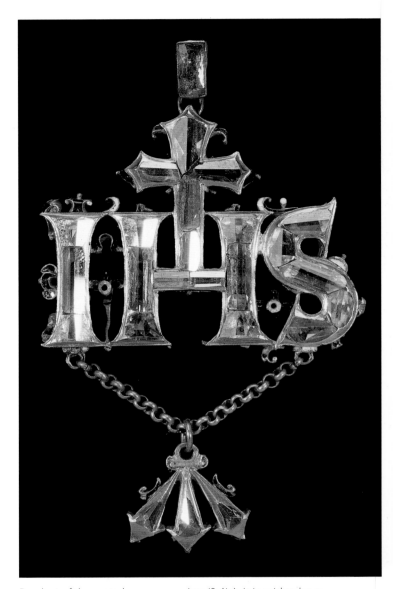

Pendant of the sacred monogram IHS, surmounted by a cross and with the three nails from the Crucifixion below, made of gold set with hog-back diamonds. Made in Northern Europe in the late sixteenth century (height 6cm/2.4in). It is said to have belonged to Sir William Howard, Viscount Stafford, who was beheaded in 1680 for alleged complicity in the Titus Oates plot. The back is enamelled with the symbols of Christ's Passion.

Left: Pendant of the pelican in its piety, made of enamelled gold set with a large foiled red paste and hung with pearls. Spanish, *c.* 1550–75 (height 8.8cm/3.5in).

Right: Pendant of enamelled gold with garnets, turquoises and pearls, and a central panel of the Flight into Egypt in *verre églomisé* (glass painted on the reverse and backed with gold foil). Made in Spain or Italy in the early seventeenth century (height 10.7cm/ 4.2in).

Above: The Tor Abbey Jewel, a dramatic *memento mori* pendant of a coffin, which opens to reveal a skeleton. Of enamelled gold, it was made *c.*1540–50 (height 8cm/3.1in). The Moresque decoration on the lid was common throughout Europe, but the inscription around it – THRONGH.THE. RESVERRECTION.OF.CHRISTE. WE.BE.ALL.SANCTIFIED – confirms the jewel's English origin. It was reputedly found in the grounds of Tor Abbey in Devon, an estate that passed into secular ownership following the dissolution of the monasteries in the 1530s.

GLORIANA

The Armada or Heneage Jewel, by tradition given to Sir Thomas Heneage – a Privy Counsellor and Vice Chamberlain of the Royal Household – by Queen Elizabeth after the defeat of the Spanish Armada, but probably slightly later, c.1595. Enamelled gold set with table-cut diamonds and Burmese rubies. On the right is the back cover, which protects the painted miniature within. The ark and the inscription, which means 'peaceful through the stormy waves', refer to Elizabeth as the defender of the English Church (height 7cm/2.8in).

Some of the finest pieces of Elizabethan court jewellery were made in celebration of Queen Elizabeth I herself, luxuriant expressions of the cult that had developed around her by the last two decades of her long reign. This cult flattered both the political and personal vanity of the queen – distracting attention from problems such as the great cost of the Spanish war, rebellion in Ireland and a series of poor harvests, and giving an air of omnipotence and a 'Mask of Youth' to the visibly ageing ruler. The pendants, with their intricately carved cameo portraits or exquisitely painted miniatures by Nicholas Hilliard, presented a reassuring vision of a calm and settled monarchy. Some were commissioned by the queen as diplomatic or personal gifts, others by individuals keen to demonstrate their devotion and loyalty – in 1586 the Earl of Rutland spent £80 on a

'brooch of her Majesties picture in an aggatt sett with 53 diamondes'. These jewels were much worn at court, and some courtiers chose to wear them prominently in their portraits (see page 34).

The finest of these historic pieces were highly complex, uniting the skills of goldsmith, gem-setter, enameller, cameo-carver and miniature painter or limner. Decorated on both sides, some also open at the back to reveal further layers of splendour within. Much simpler were the rings set with cameo portraits. These hardstone cameos of the queen were produced in significant numbers from around 1575. Some are known to have been carved by French craftsmen, but it is likely that others were produced by a London workshop.

The Armada Jewel, the Drake Jewel and the ruby-set locket all contain miniatures of Queen Elizabeth painted

The Barbor Jewel. The sardonyx cameo of the queen is framed with rubies and diamonds in an enamelled gold frame, surmounted by a crown made of three rectangular diamonds and hung with a cluster of pearls. The back is decorated with an oak tree. Family tradition claims that it was commissioned by Richard Barbor, a Protestant who escaped the stake thanks to Elizabeth's accession. However, the style of the enamelling and the Queen's costume indicate a date *c.*1600, significantly after Barbor's eventual death in 1586 (height 6cm/2.4in).

by Hilliard, the first two being concealed behind an enamelled cover at the back. Hilliard was the son of a goldsmith and himself a Freeman of the Goldsmiths' Company as well as being the leading English miniaturist of his day. As such he would have been well qualified to oversee the creation of these complicated jewels, although the extent of his involvement in their overall design and production remains a mystery. What is clear is his determination to paint accurately the jewellery worn by his sitters, which he even succeeded in making sparkle. Gold paint was a familiar material, but tiny rubies he represented using a stained resin over a layer of burnished silver and highlighted pearls with a spot of silver paint. Sadly the silver has tarnished over the years, now giving the very different effect of a black spot on each of the white pearls.

GLORIANA

Miniature portrait of Queen Elizabeth by Hilliard, flanked by the front and back of its elaborate gold locket, c.1600. The openwork front is encrusted with table-cut rubies and diamonds, with a central star representing Stella Britannis. The vividly enamelled scrollwork of the back includes stylized flowers and two pairs of dolphins (height of ruby-set lid 6.4 cm/2.5in).

The Drake Jewel, set with a sardonyx cameo of the profiles of a noble blackamoor and a white lady. The back of the jewel opens to reveal a Hilliard miniature of the queen from 1588. The gold setting has an intricate strapwork design, set with rubies and diamonds and richly enamelled in many colours. The jewel was given by Queen Elizabeth to Sir Francis Drake, perhaps after the defeat of the Spanish Armada, and he wears it in a portrait of 1591 (height 11.7cm/4.6in).

NECKLACES OF THE LATE RENAISSANCE

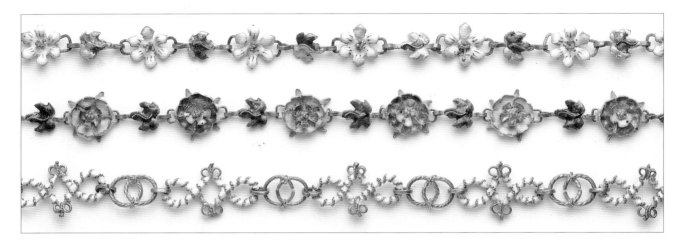

During the second half of the sixteenth century ladies' low necklines were generally superceded by high collars, perhaps lined with a small ruff or by a very deep circular ruff of luxuriant starched lace. Consequently, necklaces were more likely to be seen against a background of rich fabric than against skin, and they needed to be of a length to complement these new lines. Towards the end of the century an open square neckline returned, with the still elaborate ruffs descending down each shoulder rather than making a continuous circle. This allowed more delicate, shorter necklaces. Long necklaces continued in use, now worn inside the ruff and hanging even lower on the body.

Queen Elizabeth I is often portrayed wearing magnificent pearl necklaces, multiple strands of large and lustrous matching pearls that fall well below her waist. In 1568 she had acquired the celebrated pearls of Mary Queen of Scots – six magnificent ropes and twenty individual pearls said to be as large as nutmegs, which had been Mary's wedding gift from her mother-in-law, Catherine de' Medici. Few could rival the magnificence of Elizabeth's pearl necklaces, although Bess of Hardwick, in a portrait of 1592, wears similar ropes of pearls strikingly set against her black widow's gown.

Elaborate enamelled and gem-set necklaces continued in fashion, usually made of separate roundels of foliate openwork linked together and worn close to the neck. Long chains tended to be less densely patterned, but they too could be richly jewelled and coloured with vivid enamels. Even plain gold chains were subtly enlivened by patterning and varying the links. Decorative chains were an important aspect of male jewellery, either wrapped several times around the neck or worn long to the waist with a pendant attached, and portraits indicate that chains enjoyed a wider popularity amongst men, women and children than the few survivals would suggest. In addition to goldsmiths' work, glass chains and necklaces were commonplace in the sixteenth century, although again very few have survived. A small collection, found at the Tirolean castle of Ambras, were probably made in Innsbruck at the glass house founded by Archduke Ferdinand in 1570, but Venice would have been the principal source.

Over thirty different patterns of chains from the first decades of the seventeenth century have been preserved amongst the jewellery of the Cheapside Hoard (most of which is on display at the Museum of London). Most are of enamelled gold, although some are also set with coloured stones or pearls. The selection illustrated shows the prevalence of alternating flowers and leaves, and also the fashion for knots as a decorative motif. Such thin gold is easily damaged, and the enamel soon chips, and it is clear that these have survived only because, as unsold stock from a goldsmith's shop, they were never worn.

Above: Chains of enamelled gold from early seventeenth-century London, part of the Cheapside Hoard – thought to have been a goldsmith's stock – which was concealed beneath floorboards in the seventeenth century and only rediscovered during demolition work in 1912 (diameter of roses on centre chain 1cm/0.39in)

Chain of gold and pearls, enamelled in white, black and blue. From the imperial castle of Ambras, near Innsbruck, and probably made in an imperial workshop in Prague or Austria, c.1615. Most unusually it is marked with the maker's monogram RV on the back of each link (width of links 2.9cm/1.1in).

Chain of enamelled gold set with rubies, made in Germany, c.1620. (diameter 16cm/6.3in).

TOKENS OF LOVE

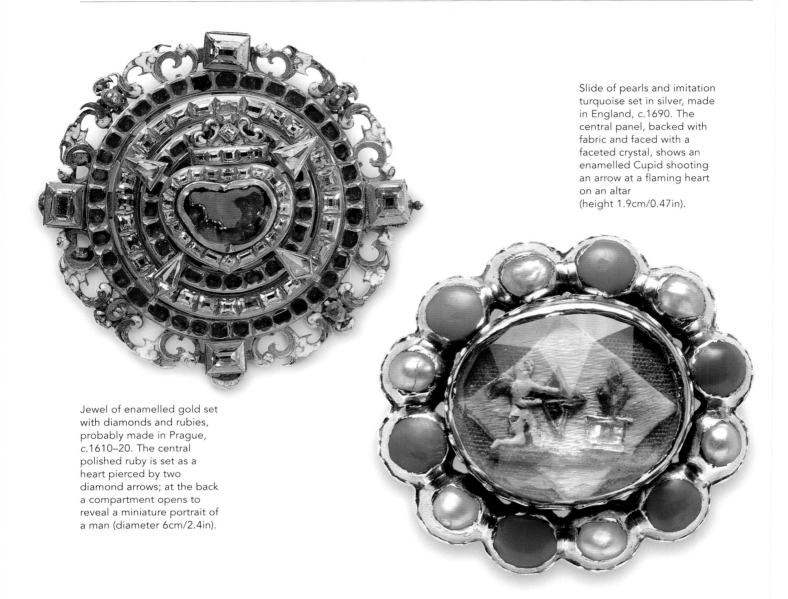

Slide of pearls and imitation turquoise set in silver, made in England, c.1690. The central panel, backed with fabric and faced with a faceted crystal, shows an enamelled Cupid shooting an arrow at a flaming heart on an altar (height 1.9cm/0.47in).

Jewel of enamelled gold set with diamonds and rubies, probably made in Prague, c.1610–20. The central polished ruby is set as a heart pierced by two diamond arrows; at the back a compartment opens to reveal a miniature portrait of a man (diameter 6cm/2.4in).

Rings have always been exchanged between lovers, and from medieval times often carried a concealed phrase or motto, known as a posy, engraved on the inside of the band. By the seventeenth century the exterior of these rings was usually plain, but there was an immense variety of inscription possible within, such as: 'In thee my choice I do rejoice', 'In love at night is my delight' and 'God above increase our love'.

In addition rings were a requirement for the wedding ceremony – although a ring might be borrowed for this and was not always worn permanently afterwards as a symbol of the marriage. Unlike the plain gold band used in modern times any style of ring could be used as a wedding ring, and they were often elaborate. The convention of wearing the wedding ring on the third finger dates from Roman times, when it was believed that a vein ran directly from there to the heart, but different hands were used at different periods. In England before the Reformation the third finger of the right hand was used, and it was only in the 1549 *Book of Common Prayer* that this was changed to the left. During the Commonwealth extreme Puritans tried to abolish wedding rings altogether, but they were firmly re-established with the restoration of the monarchy in 1660.

Above: Silver locket embossed with the figure of Cupid and inscribed around the edge NOE HEART MORE TRUE THEN MINE TO YOU. From the second half of the seventeenth century, it bears the unidentified maker's mark RA (height 2.6cm/1.02in).

Top left and centre: A German wedding ring of enamelled gold and a diamond, c.1575. The motif comes from the Italian *mani in fede*, or hands clasped in faith, and was a popular symbol of love. Double or triple interlocking hoops were known as gimmel rings, from the Latin *gemellus*, meaning twin. Concealed on the inside edges of the hoops is a German quotation from the marriage ceremony: 'What God has joined together let no man put asunder' and 'my beginning and end'.

Cupid, the cherubic but mischievous child of Venus, remained as universal a symbol of love in the seventeenth century as he had been during the Renaissance. In 1608 the Dutch artist Otto van Veen published his *Amorum Emblemata*, an emblem book, in which Cupid illustrates 124 insights into love, mostly based on quotations from Ovid. This was followed by other books of emblems, and as the genre became fashionable throughout Europe it exerted a powerful influence on jewellers and designers working across the decorative arts. Cupid's commonest pose, about to fire his arrow, has remained a much used amatory motif to this day.

Slides of the late seventeenth century frequently had a sentimental or a mourning theme. These oval jewels had two loops at the back, which ran vertically, allowing a ribbon to be threaded through them. This was then tied around the wearer's wrist or neck. Most often the central panel was of woven hair decorated either with twisted gold-wire initials and a simple garland, or with a simple figurative scene stamped out of thin sheet metal and enamelled. The central composition might be framed with a circle of pearls or stones and was protected by a faceted panel of rock crystal – which was sourced in Cornwall and near Bristol.

BODICE ORNAMENTS OF THE SEVENTEENTH CENTURY

The bodice of a gown has always provided one of the best settings for imposing jewellery. In the second and third decades of the seventeenth century a single substantial jewel worn in the centre of the bodice largely replaced the scattering of dress jewels and pendants that had been typical during the Renaissance.

The leaf-shaped diamond-set bodice ornament illustrated opposite is a fine example of the *cosse-de-pois* or pea-pod style that was fashionable in the 1620s and 1630s, and also shows the emerging dominance of the diamond over sculpted and enamelled gold. The botanical inspiration of this new style is often more easily detected in the engraved designs that survive. These are evidenced in work by designers such as Balthasar Lemercier and Jacques Caillart of Paris, and Peter Symony of Strasbourg rather than in the actual jewels, where the stylized pods, leaves and tendrils may be subsumed by the overall shape. This particular piece is constructed in three layers, which are held together from the back with tiny gold screws. The face of the flat gold back has been enamelled in black, emphasizing the depth of the piece, above this is an intricate lattice of swirling fronds and leaves, their lines picked out with rows of diamonds like peas within a pod, and finally the central rosette. There is no loop or pin by which to attach it, indicating that it would have been stitched or pinned in place, and its weight would have required a stiff fabric to support it. A similar jewel is shown in Peter Paul Rubens' portrait of his second wife, Hélène Fourment, worn at the upper edge of her bodice in the centre. With it she wears a heavy diamond-set chain that sweeps asymmetrically from the top of the jewel to her left shoulder, then back across her body to her right shoulder.

A more ebullient style of foliate decoration is combined with a ribbon bow in the diamond and topaz bodice ornament from the second half of the seventeenth century illustrated here. Jewelled bows, echoing fabric dress trimmings, were very popular from around the 1660s, with engraved designs for particularly fine bow bodice ornaments surviving by Parisian designer François Lefèbvre. At this date rose-cut diamonds were a fairly new development, and although most of the stones in this piece are table-cut, amongst them are several roses. The deep orange of the topaz has been enhanced by the placing of a

Bodice ornament and earrings set with topazes in gold and rose-cut diamonds in silver, made in the second half of the seventeenth century, perhaps in Holland. The silver-gilt back is engraved with an elaborate floral design (height 10.5cm/4.1in).

coloured foil behind each stone, a practice that continued as long as stones were set with closed backs.

An alternative style was the more linear Brandenburg, which consisted of clusters of gems arranged horizontally. Several of these might be worn together in horizontal bars down the bodice. By 1700 a different outline was emerging, roughly triangular in shape, with the upper edge of the jewel following the neckline of the gown (see page 51). From this developed the large stomacher jewels of the eighteenth century.

Bodice ornament of gold
openwork set with 208 table-
cut and triangular point-cut
diamonds and decorated
with black and white enamel,
perhaps made in Holland,
c.1630 (height 12.4cm/
4.9in).

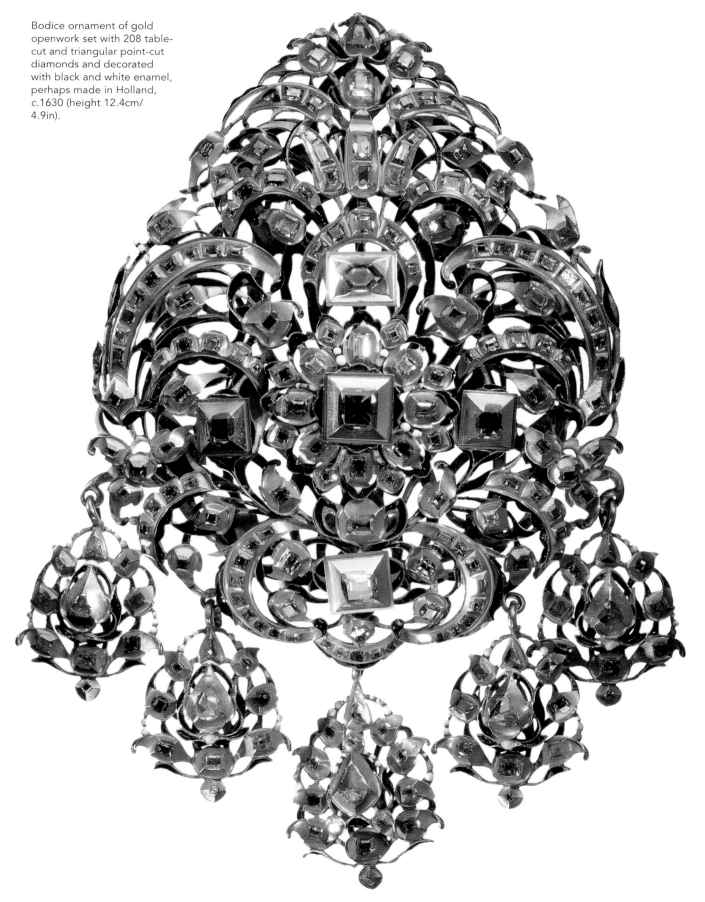

STUART JEWELLERY

Left: Portrait of Queen Anne, wife of James I, painted c.1617 by an unknown artist after the portrait by Paul van Somer. Her diamond jewellery (the diamonds painted dark grey) illustrates the new fashion for delineating pattern in stones rather than sculpting it in enamelled gold. In addition to the Sacred Monogram she wears the initials of her mother, Sophie, and her brother King Christian IV of Denmark. From contemporary books of emblems we know that the crossbow in her hair was symbolic of man's wisdom triumphing over strength.

The Stuart dynasty saw the disintegration of the great royal collection of jewels amassed by Henry VIII and Elizabeth I, beginning in a piecemeal way under James I and culminating in extensive selling and pawning of jewels to raise money for the Royalist cause during the English Civil War.

Although James was responsible for the dispersal of much of the Tudor collection, he also acquired some very fine new pieces, including the 53-carat Sancy diamond that he bought in 1604 and set as a pendant to a new jewel called the Mirror of Great Britain, which celebrated the Union of England and Scotland. His other major commission was a jewel known as the Feather, made of 26 large table-cut diamonds. Both of these pieces he wore in his hat. The tradition of New Year gifts continued at court: in 1605 the exchequer paid out £3029 to the goldsmiths Sir William Herrick and Arnold Lulls for jewels ordered by James I around the previous New Year. Lulls was an Antwerp jeweller, who is known to have been in London between 1585 and 1625. An album of jewellery drawings from his workshop dating from about 1610 has survived (see page 17).

The famous fifteenth century jewel, known as the Three Brothers, was re-set in 1623 as part of a collection of

Left: Locket, c.1610, set with a miniature of King James I, from the workshop of Nicholas Hilliard. The ark symbolizes the monarch steering the English Church through storms, a device previously used by Queen Elizabeth (height 3cm/1.2in).

Right: Royalist pendant celebrating Charles I and Charles II, c.1650–60. The gold frame has a painted enamel back with a botanical pattern and vertical loops for a ribbon for it to be worn as a slide (height 2.9cm/1.1in).

Right: Back and front of a copper-gilt locket c.1660, engraved with Charles II and Major William Carlos hiding in an oak tree at Boscobel House after their defeat at the Battle of Worcester in 1651. The coat of arms is that of the Carlos family (height 6.2cm/2.4in).

jewels that Prince Charles took to Spain in an unsuccessful attempt to woo the Infanta. Once king, he too acquired new jewels by trading in old-fashioned inherited pieces. However, the onset of the Civil War (1642–51) brought an end to such pleasures, and jewels were sold to buy arms. In 1642 Parliament legislated to protect the Crown Jewels, but this did not prevent the loss of most of the royal family's personal jewellery, including the Sancy diamond, which was pawned in Paris in 1647.

The execution of Charles I and the exile of Charles II both generated many commemorative pieces – from modest silver lockets to elaborate reliquaries – worn surreptitiously by ardent Royalists in the years before the Restoration. Rings, typically set with a miniature of Charles I, were the most common, but double portraits of father and son were also made.

On his Restoration, Charles II tried to recover pieces sold during the years of the Commonwealth, and he also arranged for a new set of regalia to be made, as the old crowns had been deliberately destroyed. Jewellery was gradually amassed again by the royal family, although there was less splendour than before at the court of William and Mary, and their successor, Queen Anne appears to have had little interest in jewellery.

RICHES FROM THE NEW WORLD

As a result of Christopher Columbus's discovery of South America in 1492 enormous quantities of gold, silver, emeralds and pearls flooded into Spain during the sixteenth and seventeenth centuries. A regular flow of trade was soon established, with ships sailing from Spain carrying manufactured goods, wine, wood, iron, cloth for the colonists and mercury, which was essential for the refining of silver. They returned with precious metals, gems, and also copper, cocoa, indigo and tobacco. Because of the danger of piracy they always sailed in convoys of six or more, escorted by at least two well-armed galleons. The other main hazard was shipwreck, and recent underwater excavations have shown how great a peril this was, and how richly laden the vessels were. The cargo of the *Nuestra Señora de Atocha*, which sank in the waters between Havana and Florida in 1622 (excavated in the mid-1980s), gives an idea of this abundance. She was carrying over a thousand bars of silver, each averaging 70 troy pounds in weight, and over 250 troy pounds of gold. A tax of 20 percent, known as the *Quinto Real* or Royal Fifth, was raised on all bullion from the Americas, providing an immense income for the Spanish Crown.

Initially the Spanish conquerors concentrated their efforts on plundering graves and temples in Peru and Mexico. Contemporary Spanish sources praised the ingenuity and beauty of the indigenous gold work, but very little survived to be admired back in Europe. Some pieces belonging to the Emperor Charles V greatly impressed Albrecht Dürer when he saw them in Brussels in 1520, but almost all this work was lost – the precious stones carefully removed and the gold reduced to gold bars for ease of shipping. In time the Spanish sought to discover the mines where the raw materials originated: gold was found in New Granada, and in 1545 they discovered the great silver mountain in Bolivia, at Potosì, which, with the forced labour of thousands of Native Americans, was to yield unbelievable quantities of silver.

Despite sustained efforts to find the source of the exceptionally deep green emeralds it was not until 1567, after great cruelty to the indigenous people, that the Spanish discovered the Muzo and Chivor emerald mines in Colombia. Colombian emeralds are still regarded as the finest, and the Muzo mine, in an extremely inhospitable jungle-like site, yielded the most prestigious shade known now as 'old mine' green. Their extraction was arduous, as explosives could not be used for risk of damaging the crystals. Spanish designs, such as the apprentice drawings of Barcelona's *Llibres de Passanties*, show the prevalence of emeralds in jewellery, but many of the most exceptional stones were sold to princely collectors in India, who spent lavishly on gems.

Above: Pendant of the Holy Inquisition, made from an emerald drop encased in an enamelled gold framework, Spanish, c.1620–30. The black and white cross is that of the Dominicans; on the back an enamelled green cross symbolizes the hope of repentance before punishment, flanked by an olive branch of reconciliation and a sword of punishment (height 4.2cm/1.7in).

Opposite top left: Pendant of emeralds set in scrolling gold foliage, made in Spain in the late seventeenth century (height 10.7cm/4.2in).

Top right: Pendant of a dragon, enamelled gold set with emeralds and rubies and hung with pearls. Probably made in the Spanish colonies in the early seventeenth century. Down his back is a spine of cabochon emeralds (height 12cm/4.7in).

Bottom: Bodice ornament of emeralds and diamonds set in gold, with enamelled flowers and insects mounted on springs that would quiver as the wearer moved. Made in Spain, c.1700 (width 14.6cm/5.7in).

As well as the Spanish, the Portuguese took full advantage of their South American colony, and chrysoberyl, a pale greenish-yellow stone found in Brazil, became a distinctive feature of Portuguese jewellery.

BOWS AND TRUE LOVERS' KNOTS, 1650–1700

Knots had been a recurring motif in jewellery since the end of the Middle Ages – their elegantly curving lines providing balanced yet subtly asymmetrical linking elements on necklaces and girdles. Perhaps the best-known English example is the series of tasselled knots on the collar of the Order of the Garter, made in gold modelled to resemble twisted rope. Throughout the sixteenth century, friars' knots – based on the three knots tied in a friar's rope belt that symbolize both the Trinity and the vows of poverty, chastity and obedience – were used in secular jewellery. More enduringly popular in jewellery was the true lovers' knot, in form rather like a 'figure of eight'. It symbolized a bond that could only be undone in death and was much used in sentimental pieces of the seventeenth century.

The knot's more frivolous relation, the bow, appears to have been a later motif in jewellery but, once established, has been used up to the present day. In the early seventeenth century ribbon bows of coloured silk were a popular dress trimming and were also used to attach a jewel to the bodice, sleeve or ruff, or as a rosette within which a small jewel might appear to greater advantage. By the middle of the century some of these fabric bows were being replaced by gem-set or enamelled bows, which soon appeared on all types of jewellery from large bodice ornaments to the small details linking the upper and lower halves of earrings. These baroque bows were usually made with double loops on each side, which drooped a little towards the end, as if the gold were imitating a soft, narrow ribbon.

The fashion for jewelled bows coincided with the spread of the new technique of painting in opaque enamels. Traditionally attributed to French goldsmith Jean Toutin of Châteaudun, it spread rapidly beyond its French origins. A wide palette was used for naturalistic flower studies and detailed figurative scenes. Equally popular was the simple but striking combination of turquoise, black and white. Painted enamel was the principal decoration for many pieces, but it was also used to add interest and colour to the backs of gem-set jewellery.

Top right: Pin or hair ornament of enamelled gold set with rubies, made in the second half the seventeenth century (height 4.6cm/1.8in).

Right: Locket of enamelled gold, set with table-cut diamonds, made in France or Spain, c.1675. The triangle at the top, which overlaps a true lovers' knot, represents the Trinity. The four upper pendants hang from further knots that terminate in an S with a bar through it, a device of both amatory and religious significance known as an *esclavos*, which as a pun combines S with *clavo* the Spanish word for 'nail', to make the word for 'slave'.

Necklace of enamelled gold, set with table-cut diamonds and hung with a pearl and a large sapphire drop, probably made in France, c.1660 (height 17cm/6.7in). Ribbons would have been attached to the gold loops at the back to fasten the necklace.

Below: Fragment of an enamelled gold chain, with medallions bearing a crowned monogram alternating with true lovers' knots. Made in France in the second half of the seventeenth century (length 16.1cm/6.3in).

EIGHTEENTH-CENTURY PASTE

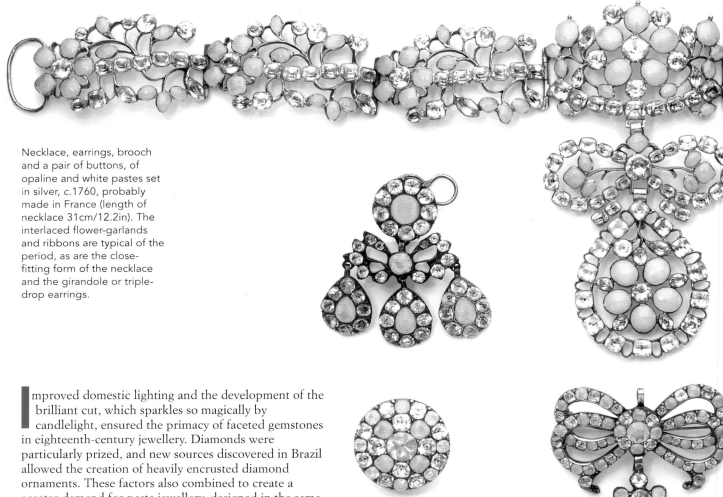

Necklace, earrings, brooch and a pair of buttons, of opaline and white pastes set in silver, c.1760, probably made in France (length of necklace 31cm/12.2in). The interlaced flower-garlands and ribbons are typical of the period, as are the close-fitting form of the necklace and the girandole or triple-drop earrings.

Improved domestic lighting and the development of the brilliant cut, which sparkles so magically by candlelight, ensured the primacy of faceted gemstones in eighteenth-century jewellery. Diamonds were particularly prized, and new sources discovered in Brazil allowed the creation of heavily encrusted diamond ornaments. These factors also combined to create a greater demand for paste jewellery, designed in the same styles but made of imitation stones of glass. Apart from cost, the great advantage of paste above precious stones was that customers were able to have 'jewels' of whatever size and shape they wanted, rather than being restricted to the family diamonds. Paste's other benefit was that it reduced the considerable anxiety of theft. All the familiar precious stones could be copied plausibly in glass, even opals, whose iridescent glow was imitated by placing a pink foil underneath a milky-blue glass.

Bohemia had developed an industry that rivalled Venice in the production of glass stones by the end of the seventeenth century, and within the next hundred years it had become the principal producer and exporter of paste stones and jewellery. In 1675 George Ravenscroft devised a recipe for lead glass that was hard enough to be faceted, and production flourished in England for the next 200 years, most notably of white pastes for buttons and buckles. However, it was France that had the greatest reputation for paste jewellery in the eighteenth century, thanks to the high-quality work of Georges Frédéric Stras from Strasbourg who pioneered this type of jewellery in Paris from the 1720s. His shop on the Quai des Orfèvres was the most famous paste jewellers, with pieces designed in the latest fashions and set in silver with as much care as if they were diamonds. Even today, paste jewellery in France is still known as *strass*.

Right: Stomacher or bodice ornament of rose-cut, foiled white pastes set in silver, probably made in England, *c.*1720 (height 23.8cm/9.4in). In some stones the underlying foil has discoloured, giving a brownish hue.

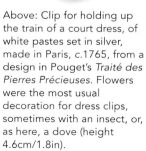

These pieces were even worn at Court in France – and in 1734 Stras was appointed jeweller to the French Crown. Similarly, in England, jewellers' trade cards show that paste was sold by many of the top jewellers – such as George Wickes, who in 1759 advertised 'False Stonework in Aigrettes, Earrings, Buckles etc'. So significant was this trade that in 1777 the English government introduced a tax of 18s. 8d. for every hundredweight of paste glass. Although of low intrinsic value, these jewels remain important historically: because over the generations so much real diamond jewellery has been broken up to be remade in the latest fashion, paste jewellery has survived in comparatively greater quantities and is a valuable indicator of changing fashions.

Above: Clip for holding up the train of a court dress, of white pastes set in silver, made in Paris, *c.*1765, from a design in Pouget's *Traité des Pierres Précieuses*. Flowers were the most usual decoration for dress clips, sometimes with an insect, or, as here, a dove (height 4.6cm/1.8in).

FASHION ACCESSORIES: SHOE BUCKLES AND CHÂTELAINES

Shoe buckles and châtelaines were two of the most widely worn items of daytime jewellery during the eighteenth century, the former of course worn by men as well as women. Both were ostensibly functional items, but they were also decorative indicators of wealth and taste, and were subject to the changing whim of fashion.

Campbell's *The London Tradesman* of 1747 comments that 'the best Branch of Buckle making is making Silver Buckles, either plain, carved or set with stones. It is a branch of the Silver-Smith's Business, and a genteel Livelihood is made of it, by working for the Shops. Those set with Stones is the Jeweller's Business and a Journeyman at either may earn from a Guinea to Thirty shillings a Week.'

During the first two decades of the century, small, rectangular buckles of silver fastened shoes high on the ankle. During the 1720s buckles began to get larger, with more variety of shape, and from the 1740s colour and sparkle were introduced with stones and paste. As the century progressed rococo scrollwork gave way to a more restrained neo-classicism, exemplified by the cut-steel buckles of the late 1770s decorated with Wedgwood jasper ware plaques. By 1790 they were falling out of use, surviving into the next century only in ceremonial and Court dress. Buckles reached their largest in the 1770s, when Sheridan's Lord Foppington in *A Trip to Scarborough* expounded that whereas buckles used to be worn to keep on the shoe 'the case is now quite reversed, and the shoe is no earthly use, but to keep on the buckle'. On a more sober note, mourning buckles were in steady demand, usually made of base metal, which was japanned or varnished black, but sometimes of faceted jet. When his mother died in 1766 Sheridan wrote from school at Harrow to his uncle for a black suit and also 'a new hat with a crape and black stokins and buckles'.

Châtelaines, known in the eighteenth century as chains or *équipages*, consist of a series of decorated and hinged panels or chains, at the top of which is a hook that attaches to the wearer's waist. From it would hang a variety of useful things – usually a matching watch or *étui* (a slender box containing miniature implements such as tweezers, folding scissors, a bodkin, a pencil and an ivory tablet, on which to write) and perhaps a watch key and seal. They were made in gold, either chased, enamelled or gem-set, as well as steel and gilt metal. Châtelaines were most widely worn during the second half of the eighteenth century but enjoyed several revivals during the nineteenth.

Opposite: Gold châtelaine and watchcase set with panels of moss agate and diamonds in silver, mid-eighteenth century (total length 19.5cm/7.7in). The watch movement is by John Pyke, and the pendant of a centaur is probably German, c.1580.

Top right: Pair of diamond and sapphire shoe buckles, made in St Petersburg, c.1750. The stones are set in silver and gold, the chapes are of steel (height 4cm/1.6in).

Right: Four English shoe buckles (clockwise from top left): mourning buckle of japanned brass commemorating the death of Queen Caroline, consort of George II, who died on 20 November 1737 aged 55; buckle of marcasites set in silver in a pattern of knotted ribbons, c.1780–90; silver and paste buckle of ribbons and rosettes, c.1780–90; silver and paste buckle, c.1760–80 (average height 4.4cm/1.7in).

JEWELLED BOUQUETS

Engraved design for a jewelled bouquet (c. 20cm/ 7.9in long), from the *Traité des Pierres Précieuses* by J. H. Pouget of Paris, 1762.

A bouquet of enamelled gold and diamonds set in silver, Spanish, from the late eighteenth century (height 22cm/8.7in). It was originally owned by Dona Juana Rabasa (wife of the Finance Minister of Charles IV of Spain), who gave it to the shrine of the Virgin of the Pillar at Saragossa.

In May 1770 the Duchess of Northumberland wrote from Paris that 'vast bouquets are quite the fashion here'. Although she was not referring specifically to jewelled bouquets, flowers were one of the most popular themes in European jewellery for most of the second half of the century, and magnificent bouquet bodice ornaments were made – sometimes up to 20 centimetres (8 inches) in length. Although only a few of these most extravagant jewels have survived, contemporary designs show that they were composed of an asymmetrical arrangement of different flowers and that their stems were usually tied with a loose ribbon bow. The petals might either be of coloured gemstones, or, for softer pastel shades, brilliant-cut diamonds were backed with coloured foils transforming them into delicate pinks, yellows and greens. The stems and foliage were often in enamel, or more lavishly in emeralds. Larger flower heads might be set on springs so that they trembled and glittered more brightly as the wearer moved, and sometimes jewelled insects were made to hover above the flowers.

A flower spray for the hair or bodice, made of densely packed rubies and diamonds with enamelled gold stems. It was made in Russia, c.1750–60, and was originally part of the Russian royal collection (height 12.6cm/5in).

Several splendid bouquets have survived in Russian collections, but otherwise they may be glimpsed only obliquely: a large diamond bouquet is listed among Queen Charlotte's jewellery, while J. H. Pouget's book *Traité des Pierres Précieuses* (1762) illustrates five substantial bouquets that he claims had been made for the Emperor. As close to the French Revolution as 1786 Queen Marie Antoinette ordered a bouquet of wild roses and hawthorn blossom from the jeweller Bapst.

On a less lavish scale garlands of jewelled flowers wrapped round with ribbons and bows were much used for necklaces, while asymmetrical sprigs or aigrettes would be pinned into the extravagant padded hair styles. Jewelled flowers twined around brooches, buckles, dress clips, earrings and miniature frames, while the style was captured in miniature by the *giardinetti*, or 'little garden' rings, where tiny blossoms were arranged with rococo asymmetry in baskets, vases and pots. The Countess of Scarborough on her marriage in 1753 was given an extensive jewel casket that included an 'aigrette of different flowers tied with a knot' and a 'small ring with flowers tyed with a knot of brilliants'.

Giardinetti, or 'little garden', rings of the mid-eighteenth century. These delicate flower compositions are studded with a variety of precious stones and paste – the diamonds are set in silver, the coloured stones in gold.

Left: State portrait of Queen Charlotte by Allan Ramsay, 1761–2. Writing in the early nineteenth century, Allan Cunningham recounts that the Crown Jewels and regalia were actually sent round to Ramsay's studio in Harley Street for him to copy, and that 'sentinels were accordingly posted day and night in front and rear of his house'.

Below: Pair of French bracelet clasps, c.1770, perhaps a gift from Marie Antoinette to one of her ladies at the time of her marriage to Louis XVI (height 5cm/2in). The blue-paste plaques are framed and ornamented with diamonds, one bears her initials and the other a trophy of love with doves and hymeneal torches.

DIAMONDS AND COURT DRESS

Diamond jewellery was an established feature of mid-eighteenth-century court life throughout Europe, and the owning and display of fine jewels was considered an essential requirement for aristocratic life. A few particularly magnificent examples from Dresden, Munich, Lisbon and St Petersburg have survived. The most splendidly bejewelled days at the English Court were the king's and queen's birthdays, when glittering receptions were held in their honour, with monarchs and nobility in their finest and most extravagant jewels. There were also many other functions both in London and the provinces when social status was reinforced by the wearing of lavish quantities of jewellery.

Queen Charlotte was famed in her day for her love of diamonds and was usually accompanied in public by their sparkle. In her portrait by the Scottish artist Allan Ramsay, the newly crowned queen wears a diamond aigrette in her hair, a close-fitting necklace of 26 large brilliant-cut diamonds, pearls around her wrists, shoulders and waist, and a diamond stomacher that fills the entire front panel of her bodice. She was the first English queen since the Civil War to have such magnificent jewellery. The Duchess of Northumberland wrote in her diary that 'the stomacher, which is valued at £60,000, is the finest piece of magnificence and workmanship I ever saw. The fond is a network as fine as cat gut of small diamonds and the rest is a large pattern of natural flowers, composed of very large diamonds.' It was made in several sections to allow the wearer a little movement.

Bracelets at this date were invariably worn in pairs, and the most typical style consisted of multiple strings of pearls fastened with a large oval clasp. Amongst George III's many gifts of jewellery to Queen Charlotte were a pair of bracelets with six strings of large pearls fastened with diamond-set clasps, one of which contained his miniature, the other his hair and cipher. The diamond-set buckles associated with Marie Antoinette show that this was also the fashion in France.

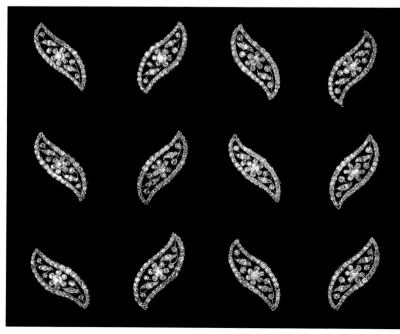

Top right: Set of bodice ornaments of brilliant-cut diamonds set in silver, from the Russian royal collection and made, c.1760, perhaps by Louis Duval of St Petersburg (width of largest bow 11.2cm/4.4in). They would have been worn together in descending size down the front of the bodice. Like the dress ornaments these were sold after the Revolution by the Bolshevik government.

Right: Twelve dress ornaments from a set of 46, made of brilliant-cut diamonds set in silver, from the Russian royal collection, c.1770, perhaps by Louis Duval of St Petersburg (average length 4.2cm/1.4in). The backs of some of the set are inscribed with royal inventory numbers, and all are edged with tiny silver holes, through which they would have been stitched to a silk gown.

MEN'S JEWELLERY

A revolving three-sided topaz fob seal, engraved with a view of the Battle of Trafalgar and (in reverse) ENGLAND EXPECTS THAT EVERY MAN THIS DAY WILL DO HIS DUTY. The deeply chased scrolls and flowers of the gold mount, c.1815, are typical of the rococo revival of the early nineteenth century (height 4.3cm/1.7in).

Opposite
Top: A freemason's ring made in England in the mid-eighteenth century of gold, silver, emeralds and rose-cut diamonds. The central shell contains Masonic emblems.

Centre: Pair of shoe buckles worn by Admiral Sir Rupert George. With inner gold rim, pastes set in silver and steel chapes, they were made in England, c.1780–90 (height 5.4cm/2.1in).

Bottom: Pair of knee buckles of pastes set in silver and steel chapes, made in England in the early nineteenth century (height 2.2cm/0.8in).

Very little survives of the most elaborate male jewellery from the second half of the eighteenth century, as the less flamboyant fashions of the nineteenth rendered it obsolete and resulted in most of it being broken up. It is clear, however, that at court gentlemen were usually as lavishly adorned as their wives. This custom extended from the highest levels such as the German Prince Carl Anselm of Thurn and Taxis, whose magnificent set of 45 diamond buttons with matching tasselled diamond buttonholes of 1775 may be seen in the Bayerisches Nationalmuseum, Munich, to the more common accessories of snuff-box, jewelled watch chain and rings that the Italian adventurer Casanova used to reinforce his image as a nobleman. Diamonds were also frequently to be seen on buckles for shoes, stocks and knee breeches, on the insignia of the many orders of chivalry, on sword hilts and on the loop and button used to fasten up the brim of a hat. The social messages conveyed by jewels were the same regardless of sex. This was underlined during the early days of the French Revolution in September 1789, when the gentlemen of the Assembly symbolically removed their gold fobs, diamond shoe buckles and other items of jewellery, and donated them to the cause of the Revolution.

By around 1800 shoe buckles had gone out of fashion, replaced by shoe strings or laces, and, with the arrival of long trousers, knee buckles too disappeared. Decorative buttons remained in regular use but became mostly much plainer and were very seldom jewelled. With the exception of jewelled orders and medals (many were honoured for services to their respective countries during the Napoleonic Wars) sparkle was largely confined to a gem-set pin fastening a shirt front or pleated cravat. Up to the 1830s colour might be added by seals, usually worn singly or in a cluster from a watch in a fob pocket. As with most jewellery for men, seals had a very practical justification at a time when all letters needed to be sealed with wax. More lavish jewellery remained in fashion in some parts of the continent, notably at the court in Vienna, where Lady Shelley recorded her surprise at seeing Hungarian noblemen wearing glittering jewels and even a necklace in 1816.

The Neo-classical interest in the antique resulted in many rings set with engraved gems. For those who could not afford antique or even contemporary hand-carved cameos and intaglios, James and William Tassie of Glasgow produced moulded-glass copies, known as tassies, cast from a vast selection of genuine engraved gems. Their catalogue of 1791 listed nearly 16,000 examples from which to choose.

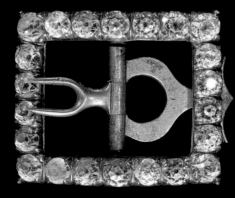
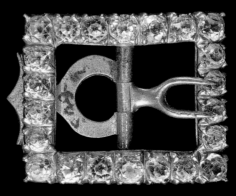

CUT STEEL

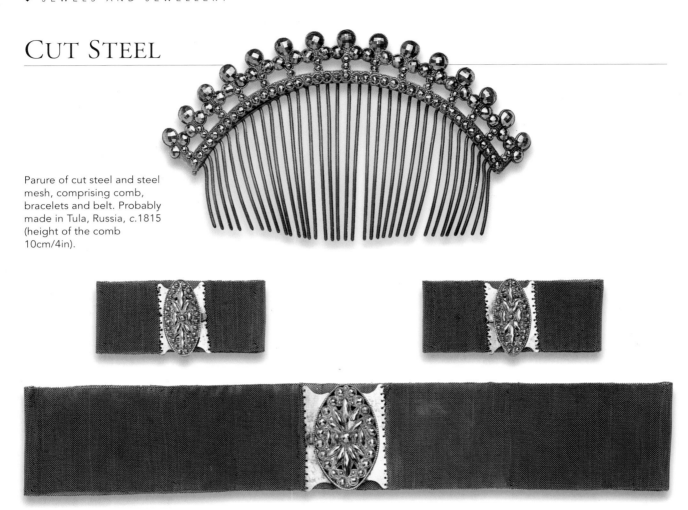

Parure of cut steel and steel mesh, comprising comb, bracelets and belt. Probably made in Tula, Russia, c.1815 (height of the comb 10cm/4in).

All manner of jewellery was made from brightly polished steel in the decades around 1800 – buckles, buttons, watch chains, necklaces, bracelets, tiaras, châtelaines, sword hilts and the star badges for orders of chivalry. Sleek pierced elements were used principally for chains and châtelaines, while in most other cases dense encrustations of bright steel studs created a surface that glittered with a dark brilliance. These were created by attaching individual faceted studs to a steel backplate, through a series of carefully spaced holes. Studs were either screwed or riveted in place: according to the diary of Sylas Neville, who visited producers in Woodstock near Oxford, in 1781, there they were screwed in place, giving a much better result than in Birmingham, where they were riveted.

The production of cut-steel ornaments appears to have first started in Woodstock in the early seventeenth century and to have spread to London, Birmingham, Wolverhampton and Salisbury by the 1760s. During the next few decades cut steel was exported widely and became part of the craze for all things English that swept France before the Revolution. By the early nineteenth

century it was also being produced in France, Italy, Spain, Prussia and Russia. Its use was not confined to those who were not able to afford more precious materials: in the inventory of the Empress Josephine's jewels made after her death, amongst a breathtaking array of gemstones were two suites of cut-steel jewellery. So fashionable was it that imitation cut steel was even made in silver, a rare survival being a comb in the V&A's collection, which was made in Birmingham in 1809. It continued to flit in and out of fashion right through the nineteenth century and was produced in Paris in small quantities until the 1940s.

One of the most important of the late eighteenth-century Birmingham manufacturers was Matthew Boulton, who collaborated with Josiah Wedgwood in combining blue and white jasper ware plaques with cut steel. He pioneered the use of steam power to drive the polishing machines and introduced an early system of mass production, described by the foreign visitor Lichtenberg in 1775, who wrote that 'each workman has only a limited range so that he does not need constantly to change his position and tools and by this means an incredible amount of time is saved.'

STEEL BUTTONS I | *Coup de Bouton*

Above: The brightness of new cut steel is sometimes hard to appreciate now. In this caricature of 1777 the lady is knocked backwards by the sun catching the cut-steel buttons on the coat of the gentleman coming towards her.

Button of cut steel set with a jasper ware plaque by Wedgwood decorated with signs of the zodiac, made in England, c.1780–90 (diameter 4.4cm/1.7in).

Right: Châtelaine of cut steel, the hook-plate decorated with a crowned monogram. Probably made in France in the early nineteenth century, with some later additions (length 52.7cm/20.7in).

SENTIMENTAL JEWELLERY: FOR LOVE AND MOURNING

Jewellery of a sentimental nature was worn by both sexes in the decades around 1800, emblems of love that might be inspired by either the dead or the living. The Neo-classical imagery of death kept its horrors at a distance, with weeping willows, broken columns, funerary urns and grieving widows replacing the stark death's heads and skeletons of earlier centuries. Mottoes such as 'not lost but gone before' and 'sacred to friendship' expressed confidence in the afterlife and joined the inscriptions detailing the name, age and date of death. In most cases black enamel was used, but for a child or unmarried person it was customary to substitute white. Mourning jewellery was usually paid for out of the deceased's estate, with details in the will as to who should be included and how much each piece should cost. Rings were the most usual type, but mourning lockets and bracelets were also sometimes made.

Locks of hair were preserved to commemorate the dead, often woven into a background panel within a mourning ring, or, less obviously, small amounts were mixed into the sepia used to paint miniature scenes on ivory or vellum. However, hair was also a reminder of the living and was exchanged between relations, close friends and lovers. In this spirit it was frequently set in more light-hearted rings and lockets or woven into a strong, slender braid suitable for a gentleman's watch chain.

A miniature portrait, worn on a bracelet clasp or within a locket, remained a popular type of love jewel, and on his death in 1830 King George IV was found to be wearing one of Mrs Fitzherbert around his neck concealed under his shirt. From the 1770s the cheaper alternative of a black-paper silhouette was introduced, mounted on an ivory background under glass and set in the same way as a painted miniature. A more enigmatic variant was the eye miniature, fashionable from the 1780s, which showed only the beloved's eye, giving little clue as to his or her identity. In addition to oval or rectangular frames, love jewels might be heart-shaped or in the form of a padlock

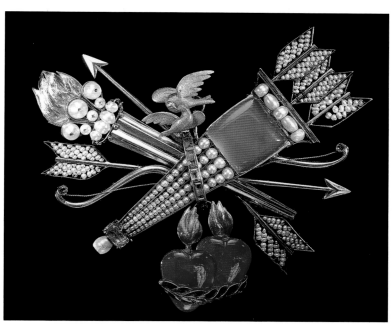

Brooch in the form of a trophy of love, with a bow and quiver full of arrows, a hymeneal torch, paired doves and two flaming hearts bound by a victor's wreath. Of gold, pearls, emeralds and cornelian, it was probably made in Paris, c.1800 (height 6.4cm/2.5in).

with an attached key – which expressed 'you have the key to my heart'. Others were framed by the motif of a serpent biting its own tail, which symbolized eternity.

The early nineteenth-century taste for polychrome jewellery was further encouraged by the 'language of stones' whereby sentiments and personal messages were spelled in gemstones by taking the initial letter of each stone used. The Empress Marie-Louise commemorated her and Napoleon's birthdays and the dates they met and married in this way. More typical were single words, such as 'love', which required lapis lazuli, opal, vermeil (an old name for garnet) and emerald, or 'dearest' spelt with diamond, emerald, amethyst, ruby, emerald, sapphire and topaz. These variously coloured stones were either set in a row across the front of a ring, or around the edges of a brooch or locket.

Opposite top left: Neo-classical mourning rings: of enamelled gold and woven hair, in memory of Gabriel Wirgman, a London jeweller, who died aged 53 in 1791; with a sepia miniature, for Martha Holworthy, who died aged 64 in 1785; opalescent enamel with painted rosebuds and inscribed 'nip't in the bud' for a two-year-old child, who died in 1792.

Right: Mourning pendant made to commemorate the death of Princess Charlotte, only child of George IV and Caroline of Brunswick, in 1817. The front is set with her portrait, by or after the royal miniaturist Charlotte Jones, the back with her coat of arms. The urn below contains her hair, arranged as Prince of Wales feathers (height including chain 9.2cm/3.6in).

Bottom: Padlock-shaped locket of coloured golds, set with a ruby, emerald, garnet, amethyst, ruby and diamond – stones whose initial letters spell the word REGARD. Made in England, c.1830–40 (height including chain 6cm/2.4in).

NAPOLEON AND JOSEPHINE

The Revolution and its aftermath had been traumatic years for French jewellery, and for most of the 1790s it had been scorned as a symbol of all that was hated about the *ancien régime*. The Parisian Corporation of Jewellers had been abolished, French diamonds had flooded the European market, and many of the craftsmen had dispersed to more lucrative centres. However, in 1799, with the establishment of the Consulate and improved stability and prosperity, jewellers began to re-establish themselves, and diamonds returned to acceptability once more. With the formal bestowing of the title of Emperor on Napoleon in May 1804, and his and Josephine's coronation in December, the revival of the luxury trades in Paris began in earnest.

Despite the Directory's sale of some of the French Crown Jewels in 1795, there were still many fine jewels in the Royal Collection, and, as Emperor, Napoleon was able to draw on these for his own use. Some were re-set to make regalia in the fashionable Neo-classical style, perhaps favoured by Napoleon for its references to the glories of the empires of Greece and Rome. Most striking was Napoleon's coronation crown by Nitot & Fils, a sparse framework of gold arches inspired by notions of Charlemagne's crown and studded with some of the finest ancient cameos and intaglios.

Engraved gems were immensely popular in the early years of the nineteenth century. In 1805 the *Journal des Dames* wrote that cameos, either ancient hardstone examples or contemporary ones carved in shell, had never been more fashionable, claiming that 'a woman of fashion wears cameos on her belt, cameos on her necklace, a cameo on each of her bracelets, a cameo on her diadem'. It was a fashion greatly encouraged by Josephine, who had not only historic stones from which to choose but also was sent contemporary examples from Italy, by Napoleon's sister Caroline Murat, whose husband had been made King of Naples in 1808.

Designs for diamonds tended to be more formal and symmetrical than those of the late eighteenth century, with Greek key pattern and the victor's wreath being typical. The convention of setting diamonds in silver and coloured stones in gold continued, but the development of 'transparent' or open-back settings some time around 1800 allowed more light through the stones. Another distinctive feature of gem-set jewellery at this date was the encircling of large coloured stones with smaller diamonds.

Jewellery was one of Josephine's favourite extravagances, and she invariably spent much more than her annual allowance. At her divorce in 1810 she had to relinquish all pieces that were considered Crown Jewels but retained a vast personal collection of immense splendour made up of gifts and purchases that included her coronation diadem of 1040 diamonds. For his second wife, Marie-Louise Archduchess of Austria, Napoleon had to commission a whole new collection of jewellery, including a parure of rubies and diamonds from Nitot & Fils for their wedding. To this he added many other jewels including a diamond parure that incorporated some larger stones from the Crown Jewels and, to mark the birth of his son the King of Rome in 1811, a diamond necklace with diamond drops, which survives in the collection of the Smithsonian Institution in Washington.

Right: Spray of laurel, of rubies and diamonds set in silver and gold. It was made for the Empress Josephine in France, c.1805, and was probably intended to be worn as a bodice ornament (length 17.2cm/6.8in).

Opposite: Necklace and earrings of emeralds and diamonds in open-back silver and gold settings. Part of a parure probably made by Nitot & Fils in 1806 and given by Napoleon and Josephine to their adopted daughter Stéphanie de Beauharnais on her marriage to the heir of the Grand Duke of Baden (height of earrings 5.5cm/2.2in). The rear emerald drops, which detach as earrings, are later.

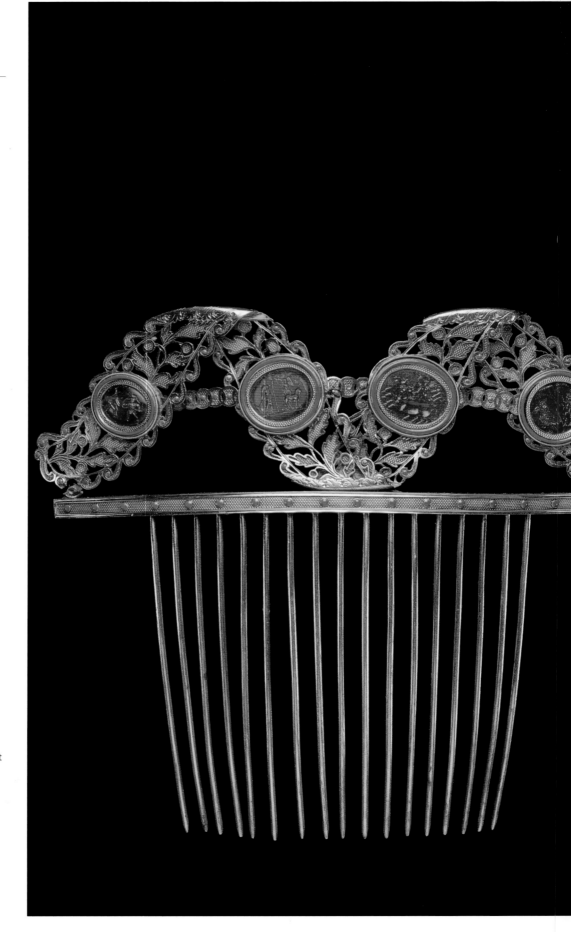

Diadem, brooch, comb and
earrings of enamelled gold
set with cornelian intaglios,
made in Paris, c.1808 (height
of comb 11cm/4.3in). These
exquisite examples of First
Empire jewellery are
believed to have belonged
to Josephine, a gift from
Napoleon's sister Caroline
Murat, who was Queen
of Naples.

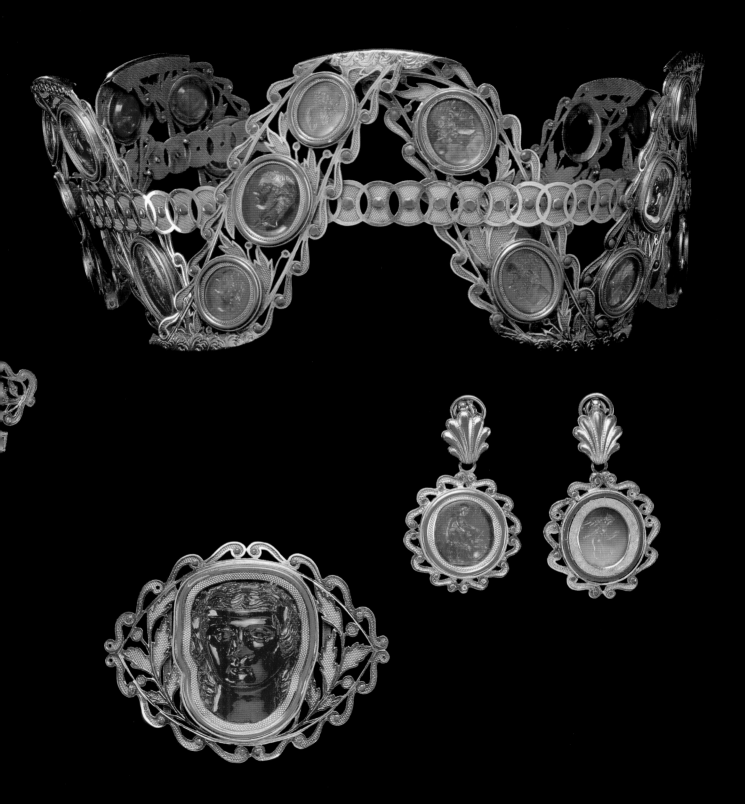

BERLIN IRON

Comb of Berlin iron, with a cast cameo of Iris in the gallery, c.1820 (height 15.5cm/6.1in).

The surprising transformation of cast iron – a dark metal of little value – into intricate objects of luxury and fashion was a Prussian success of the early nineteenth century. This delicate jewellery, resembling black lace, was produced by the Prussian Royal Iron Foundries from about 1806. Technically it required very fine or pulverized sand for casting, an addition of phosphorus to the pure molten iron and a level of care previously accorded only to precious metals. This was matched by the skills of superb designers, the most distinguished being Siméon Pierre Devaranne, Moritz Geiss and Karl Friedrich Schinkel.

The most important of the Royal Foundries was founded in 1804 in Berlin, about eight years after the first at Gleiwitz in Silesia. They were part of a government initiative to stimulate industrial and economic growth, and were greatly influenced by English innovations in smelting and casting. The production of jewellery was only a minor part of their output – secondary to industrial products, canons and munitions – and it was labour intensive, requiring a team of designers, modellers, sand moulders, colourers and chemists.

In 1806 the Prussian defeat by Napoleon resulted in Berlin being occupied, the iron foundry plundered and Napoleon removing patterns to Paris with the aim of beginning production there. There followed a brief period of stagnation until the Wars of Liberation (1813–15), although in 1810 iron ornaments were made in memory of Queen Luise, who had died that year, elegantly combining fashion and mourning. Ironically it was the wars against Napoleon that gave the greatest stimulation to the fashion for Berlin iron, following appeals by members of the Prussian royal family for citizens to donate gold jewellery to the war effort, in return for which they would be given iron jewellery. In Berlin alone it has been claimed that over 160,000 rings were exchanged. Many of these pieces can be identified by inscriptions on the back such as *Gold gab ich für Eisen*, meaning 'I gave gold for iron'. This indigenous material, noted for its strength, came to symbolize nationalism and patriotism in the struggle against the enemy, and this was epitomized when the highest Prussian honour, named the Iron Cross, was designed by Schinkel in 1813.

Berlin iron jewellery remained fashionable until the mid-1830s but continued in production into the second half of the nineteenth century and was shown at the Great Exhibition of 1851 in London. Neo-classical designs set with iron cameos and acanthus leaves were common, but equally typical were the Gothic Revival patterns of architectural tracery and also naturalistic themes of fruit and flowers. Component parts were cast in separate flat units and then linked together mechanically, which enabled some mixing of styles during assembly. Its distinctive colour was achieved by treating the new, hot castings with 'linseed cakes', which carbonized as the oil evaporated, leaving a black coating on the metal.

Right: Necklace of Berlin iron with Gothic tracery and foliage, c.1820–30 (height of trefoil units 4.6cm/1.8in). The centre of each of the larger elements is set with a reflective disc of polished steel.

Below: Earrings of Berlin iron, probably made by Devaranne of Berlin to a design c.1815 and shown at the Great Exhibition of 1851 (height 7.6cm/3in).

SOUVENIRS OF THE GRAND TOUR

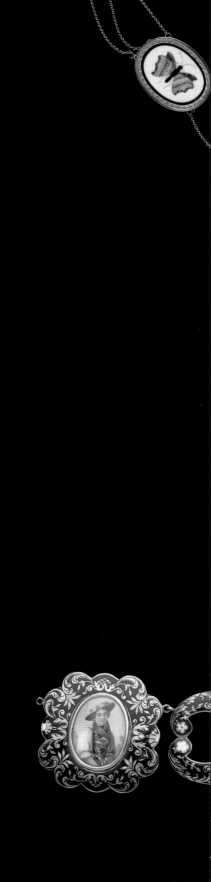

With the defeat of Napoleon and the restoration of the Bourbon kings in 1814, travel on the continent became possible for the English once again, and the steady flow of visitors to France, Italy and Switzerland recommenced. Italy was the most popular destination for tourists, and paintings and sculptures – often copies of great masterpieces – were the most celebrated purchases, but they also brought back substantial quantities of jewellery.

Visitors to Rome brought back shell cameos, miniature mosaic panels and 'Roman pearls'. Cameo-carving on both hardstone and shell was an established Roman speciality, with subjects taken from ancient gems and from paintings and sculpture. Miniature mosaics (now known as micromosaics) were originally the preserve of the Vatican workshops, but, by 1817, according to Scottish traveller Charlotte Eaton, there were 'hundreds of artists, or rather artisans, who carry on the manufactory of mosaics on a small scale ... all the streets leading to the Piazza di Spagna, are lined with the shops of these *Musaicisti*'. Minute subtly coloured tesserae, usually cut from thin glass rods, were arranged in mastic or cement on a glass panel using pointed tweezers. When all were in place, the gaps were filled with coloured wax and the surface polished. Although birds and flowers were popular subjects, the most typical motifs were the buildings and ruins of Rome. Most were bought as panels, to be mounted as jewellery or in box lids when the traveller returned home. 'Roman pearls' were clever imitations, made of alabaster that had been waxed and then dipped in a pearlescent liquid made from the entrails of a local fish. By the mid-nineteenth century, although these were all still available, they had been overtaken in prestige by the archaeological-style jewellery of the Castellani firm.

Of the other Italian cities, Florence specialized in the production of *pietre dure* or hardstone mosaics, which, like the miniature mosaics, were usually bought as unmounted panels and made up into jewellery by London or Parisian craftsmen. Naples produced jewellery in coral, 'lava' and tortoiseshell. The so-called lava, which came in a range of earthy colours from terracotta to olive green, was a coloured limestone, and it was usually carved as cameos. Venice was known for its fine gold chains, which were described by the Revd T. H. White in 1840 as being made from metal 'scarcely so thick as ladies' netting silk'.

The route to Italy lay through Switzerland, which had a long tradition of fine painting in enamel. Particularly favoured by travellers were picturesque views of the Swiss countryside and depictions of women wearing different styles of Swiss regional costume.

Top: Festoon necklace, *c.*1805, set with hardstone or *pietre dure* mosaics of moths. The mosaics were a Florentine speciality, but the fine foliate chasing of the gold suggests that the necklace was made up in France (unfastened length 40cm/15.7in).

Centre left: Shell cameo brooch of Ariel riding on a bat's back, probably carved in Italy, *c.*1830 (height 5.8cm/2.3in). The subject is taken from Shakespeare's *The Tempest*, and its treatment closely resembles a painting of 1826 by the artist Joseph Severn, long resident in Rome, which is also in the V&A's collection.

Centre right: Brooch of silver-gilt filigree set with a micromosaic panel of a bird, made in Italy, *c.*1815 (height 4.2cm/1.7in).

Bottom: Part of a necklace made of painted enamel plaques showing folk costumes of the Swiss cantons, made in Switzerland, *c.*1830 (height of the first panel 2.7cm/1.1in).

JEWELLERY OF THE 1820S AND 1830S

Portrait of Elizabeth, Lady Stuart de Rothesay, and her daughters, painted by Sir George Hayter in 1830–31. Lady Stuart de Rothesay was the wife of the British Ambassador to Paris. The bandeau beneath her turban, her earrings, necklace, belt buckle, bracelets and rings show the contemporary taste for mixing colours and forms.

filigree core. The spirals were known as *cannetille* work, the granules as *grainti*. An alternative texture can be seen on the vine leaves of the necklace opposite, where a stippled surface was created using a metal point. The general effect was much bulkier and heavier than the Neo-classical jewellery from the turn of the century. However, this impression is somewhat deceptive, as the pieces are usually very light, cleverly achieving an opulent effect with the minimum of gold.

Low, sweeping necklines favoured substantial necklaces, and fitted bodices were now separated from bell-shaped skirts by deep waistbands – for which tall, slender buckles were required. Long chains were fashionable, falling below the waist and sometimes with an eyeglass, scent bottle or vinaigrette (a small box containing a sponge soaked in aromatic essences) attached as a pendant. The arrival of puffed sleeves encouraged the wearing of large bracelets: as *Townsend's Monthly Selection of Parisian Costumes* noted in February 1826 'the rage for bracelets still continues. To multiply the number, a lady of fashion does not object to sacrifice the beauty of her arms, by covering them with cameos and stones, from the wrists to the elbows.' Likewise it became fashionable to wear a stack of different rings all on one finger. Earrings were long, with the *Ladies Magazine* of 1828 commenting that 'the length of ear pendants is indeed remarkable'. They were invariably for pierced ears, a delicate operation usually carried out by the jeweller. A new and distinctive style of head ornament was the *ferronière* – consisting of a single jewel worn on the forehead, suspended on a delicate chain or cord. It was named after Leonardo da Vinci's painting *La Belle Ferronière*, which features a similar piece. Also typical of the period were turbans, which gave rise to slender bandeaux worn at their base, and a variety of jewels that could be pinned on to them.

Although cameos remained fashionable, Neo-classical lines were in general replaced by the more extravagant rococo revival style. The rise of Romanticism engendered a powerful interest in the Middle Ages and Renaissance, resulting in historicist and heraldic ornament being used in jewellery, while at the same time naturalistic motifs such as vines, flowers and foliage enjoyed a return to favour.

Jewellery from these decades was colourful and flamboyant, with increased availability of amethysts, garnets, peridots, chrysoprases, topazes and turquoises to augment the designer's palette. Gems were set in rich gold surrounds either as a series of large stones all of the same colour, or massed together in an apparently random, multicoloured assortment. Gold settings were typically either stamped out of sheet-gold – when they were smooth and brightly polished – or consisted of encrustations of spirals and granules on a

Detail of a necklace made of coloured gold and pearls, in a naturalistic pattern of vines. Probably made in England between 1835 and 1845 (height of centre section 6cm/2.4in).

Below: Bow brooch of gold filigree with *cannetille* and *grainti* decoration, set with turquoises and pearls, *c.*1825 (width 5.5cm/2.2in).

Right: Brooch and pair of earrings of stamped gold and cabochon garnets, made in England, *c.*1835 (height of brooch 6.9cm/2.7in).

MID-CENTURY NATURALISM

Precise naturalistic jewellery, decorated with clearly recognizable flowers and fruit, emerged with the Romantic movement in the early nineteenth century and remained popular for many decades. Examples from the 1820s and '30s were typically small, delicate sprigs, but by the middle years of the century these had developed into much more extravagant and complex compositions. The style owed its success to the intrinsic prettiness and wearability of jewelled flowers and foliage and to the enduring enthusiasm for botany. The introduction of exotic plants to Europe, although not a new phenomenon, continued to fascinate long into the century, facilitated by the development of hot-houses, while new varieties such as the pansy were being bred for garden use from wild flowers. Roses, fuchsias,

chrysanthemums and dahlias were amongst the most fashionable garden plants of the mid-nineteenth century, and these flowers, along with many others, became frequently used motifs in jewellery.

Meanings were commonly attached to particular plants, and as a result a jewel might also symbolize a noble characteristic or sentiment: for example the forget-me-not signified true love; the lily of the valley, a return of happiness; ivy, friendship and fidelity. Floral jewellery therefore made touching gifts of love or friendship. Prince Albert gave Queen Victoria several pieces of jewellery decorated with white-porcelain orange blossom, gold leaves and tiny enamelled green oranges between 1839 and 1846. Here the symbolism worked on two levels, the orange blossom declaring that the Queen's

Opposite: Diamond bodice ornament, c.1850, shaped as a bouquet of mixed flowers including roses, a carnation, a chrysanthemum and a fuchsia – some of which are on springs to increase their glitter as the wearer moves. The three sprigs of berries on the right-hand side have been incorporated from an earlier piece (length 28cm/11in).

Above: Necklace of carved amethyst grapes and enamelled-gold vine leaves,

c.1840–50 (height of central unit 8cm/3.1in). Compare this vivid colouring with the more delicate necklace of pearl grapes and coloured gold foliage on page 77.

Right: Brooch, c.1845–50, in the form of a spray of convolvulus, with petals of pavé-set turquoises and pearl stamens (height 12.5cm/4.9in). In the language of flowers the convolvulus symbolized 'bonds' or 'extinguished hopes'.

purity was equalled by her loveliness and the four ripening fruit representing their young children.

A variety of different materials could be used to match the colours in nature: white berries were carved in chalcedony, red ones in cornelian or coral, while entwined branches and leaves were often of coloured gold or enamelled. A more costly alternative was to set entire bouquets with precious stones. Many of the finest of these glittering floral jewels were shown at the Great Exhibition of 1851, when even the Parisian jeweller François-Désiré Froment-Meurice, known as the champion of the historical revival, included a large diamond and ruby bouquet of roses, rosebuds, convolvulus and fuchsia in his display. The French Empress Eugénie was particularly fond of naturalistic jewellery and in the mid-1850s had diamonds from the French crown jewels re-set as a parure of currant leaves and berries.

THE GREAT EXHIBITION, 1851

The 'Great Exhibition of the Industry of All Nations' in London's Hyde Park was an extraordinary phenomenon that brought together the manufactures, machinery, raw materials and fine arts of Britain and her Empire, and those of 34 other countries from across the world. Covering an area of over 19 acres and housed in what became known as the Crystal Palace, it was seen by an estimated six and a half million visitors – equivalent to almost 30 percent of the population of the United Kingdom at that time. Jewellery was featured in an immense variety of styles and materials – from the technical sophistication of the grand jewellery houses to the simple shell necklaces worn by Tasmanian aborigines.

Many European jewellers exhibited extravagant naturalistic jewellery, with lifelike arrangements of jewelled flowers tied with diamond ribbons (see page 78). Hunt & Roskell of London created one of the most elaborate bouquets using around 6000 diamonds. The Parisian Gabriel Lemonnier's parure for Queen Christina, the Spanish queen mother – with its diamond flowers, pearl buds and emerald leaves – was, according to the *Illustrated London News*, 'one of the most attractive displays in the building'. St Petersburg jewellers too were working in this style and were particularly commended for the delicacy of their settings.

Much more to the taste of the artistic establishment was historicist jewellery, inspired by medieval and Renaissance models, which often combined architectural and figurative ornament. The French goldsmiths Froment-Meurice, patronized by Queen Victoria and Prince Albert, and Rudolphi were particularly noted for this style of work. The English designer A. W. N. Pugin included jewellery with strong ecclesiastical resonances in his Medieval Court. His commitment to the techniques as well as the motifs of the Middle Ages is indicated by the *champlevé* enamel and cabochon stones, and he was greatly distressed when this was undermined by the unauthorized use of anachronistic split pearls and highly polished gold by his Birmingham manufacturer. The Frenchman Félix Dafrique revived Renaissance *commesso* work, where a very rich effect was created by applying enamelled gold and

A shell cameo of Queen Victoria with enamelled gold robes, and jewelled regalia. This *commesso* brooch is by Dafrique, whose 'polychromatic cameos' gained him a prize medal. The cameo is after Thomas Sully's 1838 portrait of Queen Victoria and is signed on the reverse 'Paul Lebas/ Graveur/1851/Paris' (height 6.1cm/2.4in).

gemstones to a cameo. Also of antiquarian interest were the copies of Irish ring brooches from the seventh and eighth centuries, which were shown by two Dublin firms, and which became popular as shawl fasteners.

Although more fashionable earlier in the century, Berlin iron jewellery won praise in 1851 for both its artistic and technical intricacy, while cut steel was shown by firms from London, Birmingham and Paris. Cable bracelets of woven hair were exhibited by Benjamin Lee of London. Regional specialities included Bohemian garnets, Italian coral, Whitby jet and Irish bog-oak. Scottish pebble jewellery was exhibited by Rettie & Son of Aberdeen, while Edinburgh firms showed plaid brooches for highland dress. A fascinating but far less comprehensive selection of non-European jewellery was displayed, including Turkish pieces in silver and gold and Tunisian folk jewellery. More significant was the collection of Indian jewellery contributed by the East India Company.

Important gemstones were also exhibited, notably two of the world's most famous diamonds – the Koh-i-noor and the deep blue Hope Diamond – both of which attracted huge crowds. The Hope Collection of gems included the largest known pearl, which was 2 inches long and 4.5 in diameter, while an equally fascinating curiosity, a black diamond of 350 carats, was exhibited by Joseph Mayer.

Right: Headband, necklace and brooch from Pugin's extensive parure designed in 1848 for his third wife – Pugin wrote 'no woman, not excepting the Queen, will have better ornaments as regards taste.' It was displayed in the Medieval Court at the Great Exhibition, an area devoted to contemporary applications of medieval art (height of brooch 5.4cm/2.1in).

Above: A copy of the Royal Tara brooch exhibited by the Dublin jeweller G. & S. Waterhouse (height 6.8cm/2.7in). This adaptation of oxidized silver, partially gilded and set with diamonds, amethysts and river pearls, was shown alongside the larger original that had been discovered the previous year near Drogheda.

Left: According to the Art Journal Illustrated Catalogue, 'The visitor to the Great Exhibition may search in vain ... for works more truly beautiful of their class, than those contributed by M. Froment-Meurice.' This bracelet of silver cherubs amidst gilded and enamelled foliage was bought directly from the Exhibition for £18 (length 18.1cm/7.1in).

THE ARCHAEOLOGICAL STYLE

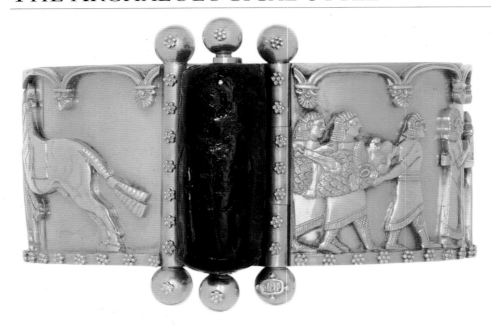

Above: Bracelet of gold with a steatite cylinder seal clasp, by John Brogden, c.1860. It shows the Assyrian King Ashurbanipal sacrificing on his return from a lion hunt (height of seal 3cm/1.2in).

Opposite top: Necklace with a mask of Achelous, made by Carlo Giuliano, c.1865 (height of mask 5.4cm/2.1in).

Centre: Russian jeweller Carl Fabergé's copies of Greek jewellery from the Crimea were exhibited in Moscow in 1882 to great acclaim. This bracelet with star-sapphire and star-ruby terminals, c.1908–17, shows the enduring popularity of the archaeological style (width 7.2cm/2.8in). For details of the hallmarks see page 143.

Bottom: Necklace of woven gold with a fringe of hollow pendants and rosettes, made by Castellani, c.1870 (length 35cm/15.4in). It is copied from a Greek original, c.360 BC, which was excavated at Kul Oba in the Crimea in 1864.

In 1863 William Burges commented: 'It is only since our workmen have taken to imitating the beautiful articles found in the tombs of Etruria and Magna Graecia that an artist can pass a jeweller's shop without shutting his eyes.' Archaeological jewellery, often closely copied from surviving finds, was particularly admired in intellectual circles from around 1860 until at least the late 1880s as a welcome relief from the opulence of diamond-encrusted naturalism.

Unlike the Neo-classical jewellery from the years around 1800, by the third quarter of the century there was an informed understanding of the forms and decoration of ancient jewellery thanks to archaeological discoveries across the ancient world. For the first time these intricate gold ornaments were collected, studied and published, and they exerted a powerful fascination. Although the jewellers' determination to replicate them accurately may now appear derivative, at the time the style was considered highly innovative. The pieces were very exacting technically, highly labour-intensive and prompted endless experiments to rediscover forgotten techniques. Most elusive of these techniques was the Etruscan art of granulation, where a fine texture or pattern was created by applying minute grains of gold to a gold surface without using any solder. This technique was not mastered by nineteenth-century goldsmiths, although they achieved a similar effect with solder.

As with the ancient originals, gold was the principal and often the only material in a piece. Faceted gemstones were rarely used except by Parisian jeweller Eugène Fontenay, whose less purist designs often incorporated diamonds. Colour might be added with cameos, enamel, carved scarab beetles, an occasional cabochon stone or (for pieces in the Roman style) a micromosaic plaque. Etruscan and Greek models were most influential, but other civilizations, such as the Assyrians and the Egyptians, provided further inspiration. From 1848 Sir Austen Henry Layard's well-illustrated account of excavations at Nineveh was an important design source for jewellers, and at the Great Exhibition of 1851 two London firms, Hunt & Roskell and Garrard & Co., exhibited work in the Assyrian style. Egyptian motifs predominated at the Paris Exhibition of 1867, fostered by Auguste Mariette's excavations and the building of the Suez Canal.

Fortunato Pio Castellani with his sons Alessandro and Augusto were the acknowledged leaders of the archaeological style. Although primarily jewellers, they also collected, restored and dealt in antiquities. Their shop in Rome – lined with shelves of antique vases and cases of gold jewellery – was sufficiently famous for them to be satirized in the London magazine *Punch* (June 1859) and celebrated by Browning in his poem *The Ring and the Book*. In the early 1860s they opened shops in Naples, Paris and London, and around this time the style was adopted by many of the world's leading jewellers.

THE RENAISSANCE REVIVAL

Left: Portrait of Elizabeth, Lady Seaton, by Edward Long, 1884. Lady Seaton had the rare advantage of a magnificent sixteenth-century pendant among her family jewels: at her neck she wears the Drake Jewel (see page 41) on a rope of pearls.

Above: Necklace in the seventeenth-century style, made of silver gilt, garnets, emeralds, pastes and pearls, and paint imitating enamel, by Schlichtegroll of Vienna (length 38.1cm/15in). Part of a set that was mass-produced from standardized component parts and shown at the Paris Exhibition of 1855, from where it was purchased by the museum.

Right: Pendant of enamelled gold set with rubies, sapphires and pearls, made by Giuliano, c.1865 (height 10cm/3.9in). The onyx cameo is of Marie de Médicis, the sixteenth-century queen of France, and was engraved by Georges Bissinger after a cameo in the Cabinet des Médailles, Paris.

Opposite left: Mermaid pendant by Louis Wièse, c.1890. In the Renaissance manner, it has a baroque pearl at its centre, with enamelled gold to complete the form. On her spiralling double tail, which is set with table-cut diamonds, stands a figure of Cupid (height 8.3cm/3.3in)

Opposite right: Pendant by Froment-Meurice, c.1850–55. The coral cameo of Bacchus is encircled by a gold frame decorated with sirens (height 10.1cm/ 4in). It has two matching brooches set with cameos of Apollo and Venus.

The Romantic movement of the first half of the nineteenth century gave rise to a historicism that influenced all the decorative arts. Medieval tracery had featured Berlin iron jewellery as early as the 1820s (see page 73), and Renaissance themes followed around 1829 when Bapst re-set some of the French Crown Jewels for the Duchesse de Berri's Mary Stuart quadrille. During the 1830s the Renaissance-inspired *ferronière*, a jewel worn on a ribbon on the forehead, became fashionable across Europe, while in Paris Jean-Bapiste and Jules Fossin, and Charles Wagner pioneered more elaborate historicist jewellery. Their lead was taken up in the 1840s and '50s by Froment-Meurice, Rudolphi and Jules Wièse (whose son Louis was to carry the style into the 1900s). This more figurative work required fine modelling and goldsmithing rather than conventional gem-setting skills, while enamelling, scarcely a feature in the previous decades, was reintroduced and perfected.

In London the first major example of Renaissance-inspired jewellery was Hancock's Devonshire Parure of

1856. Its vividly banded enamel decoration influenced many designers around the time of the London Exhibition of 1862, creating a style that became known as 'Holbeinesque'. For Castellani and Giuliano the production of Renaissance revival jewellery combined well with the archaeological style, and it soon became an integral part of their work. London jewellers benefited from the exhibition of Tudor and Stuart portraits held in 1866 at the V&A (then called the South Kensington Museum). It both helped to popularize the style and provided valuable inspiration through the many detailed depictions of jewellery in the paintings.

Collectors with serious antiquarian leanings might try to acquire genuine Renaissance jewels, although it was not always easy to avoid the fakes that were on the market from an early date. In 1842 Prince Albert gave Queen Victoria what he believed to be a complete Renaissance parure for Christmas. Modern analysis has shown that although a little of it dates back to the seventeenth century, most is from the nineteenth. Some of the most misleading of these nineteenth-century jewels were produced between 1853 and 1890 by the skilled restorer and faker Reinhold Vasters of Aachen. His working drawings are preserved at the V&A.

THE INFLUENCE OF JAPAN AND INDIA

Japanese art and design had scarcely been seen in most of Europe between 1624, when the Japanese had closed their ports to all foreign vessels except the Dutch, and the 1850s. Consequently, the Japanese Court at the London Exhibition of 1862, which was the first significant showing of contemporary Japanese work in Britain, generated immense interest. It directly influenced Lucien Falize, who, inspired by oriental cloisonné enamels, returned to Paris determined to master this technique and apply it to his jewellery. The resulting brightly coloured and distinctive enamels, with *cloisons*, or partitions, in gold rather than the traditional copper, usually drew their motifs from Japanese prints, although Indian (see page 89) and Persian patterns were also used.

The Japanese had almost no tradition of jewellery-making, their only comparable ornaments being decorative hairpins and combs, lacquered inro boxes, which hung from the belt, and Samurai sword fittings. However, their metalsmiths were highly skilled and used to working on a small scale. When the wearing of swords was banned in Japan in 1876, many armourers turned to making jewellery for export to Europe. They used dark alloys unknown in the West, which they inlaid with contrasting gold and silver: the blue-black *shakudo*, made of copper with a small amount of gold, and *shibuichi*, made of copper and silver, in shades of grey and brown. As with all new fashions they were imitated by Birmingham manufacturers, who did not attempt to replicate their complex alloys but used silver with details added in coloured golds – a combination that better suited British hallmarking regulations.

The arts of India were better known in Europe, and Indian jewellery at the Great Exhibition was richly praised by Owen Jones for possessing an integrity he felt had been completely lost in the mechanized production of the West. Its greatest appeal was in artistic circles, although Queen Victoria, Empress of India from 1876, gave Indian jewellery to Princess Alexandra as part of her wedding present in 1863.

Both Japanese and Indian jewellery was sold in aesthetic shops in London. As early as 1862, Arthur Liberty had persuaded his then employers Farmer & Rogers' Great Shawl & Cloak Emporium to buy up all that was left of the original Japanese Court. In 1875 Liberty founded his own shop, where he continued to specialize in oriental wares, by which point he was in competition with a number of department stores.

Below: Necklace of cloisonné enamel and gold by Alexis and Lucien Falize with the enameller Antoine Tard, made in Paris, *c*.1867. The clear outlines of the pattern are due to the framework of gold *cloisons* that contain the different colours of enamel flux (diameter of largest medallion 3.5cm/1.4in).

Above: Reversible green and red necklace of enamelled gold and pearls, made by Robert Phillips for the Paris Exhibition of 1867. Phillips was known to seek inspiration in museums and in this case took the motif on the palmettes from a Mughal thumb ring in the collection of the V&A (diameter 15.6cm/6.1in).

Below: Early nineteenth-century Japanese pouch fittings, mounted as a bracelet in Europe, c.1880. The panels are made of *shakudo* and gold, attached together with silver hinges and fittings (length 18.7cm/7.4in).

THE LOCKET

The Locketomanie

Lockets ... are considered indispensable with morning costumes.
QUEEN MAGAZINE, 16 DECEMBER 1871

Pendants containing a portrait miniature or a lock of hair have proved to be amongst the most enduring of jewels and most charming of mementoes. Although by no means an innovation of the second half of the nineteenth century, lockets – in which the keepsake is concealed either at the back or within the piece – became particularly popular as daytime ornaments from the 1860s to the 1880s.

London jeweller E. W. Streeter offered a typical selection. In his catalogue of 1871 he advertised over 30 different oval gold lockets, all made by machine, and ranging in price from £1 up to £50. The simplest were of embossed gold, the decoration and the body being stamped in one action by the same die. The cheapest had glass backs, in contrast with the gold-backed 'double box' lockets with their two internal compartments. Crosses were a frequently recurring decoration, and the monogram AEI (which stands for amity, eternity and infinity as well as being the Greek word for forever) was also popular. Enamel could be added to enliven the gold for £1 extra, and for more extravagant customers Streeter offered lockets decorated with diamond stars and gem-set flowers and insects. Streeter's gold lockets reflected conventional taste and were to remain popular for many years – almost two decades later most of the same designs still featured in his catalogue, which by then also offered lockets with diamond monograms costing from £30 to £200.

Lockets were considered suitable presents for bridesmaids, and Princess Louise, like many of her contemporaries, gave a locket to each of her attendants when she married in March 1871. The custom was so widespread that Streeter advertised a ten-per-cent reduction on bridesmaids' lockets when ordered in multiples of six. The commemorative nature of lockets also made them ideal jewels for mourning use when enamelled in black or carved from dark onyx or jet.

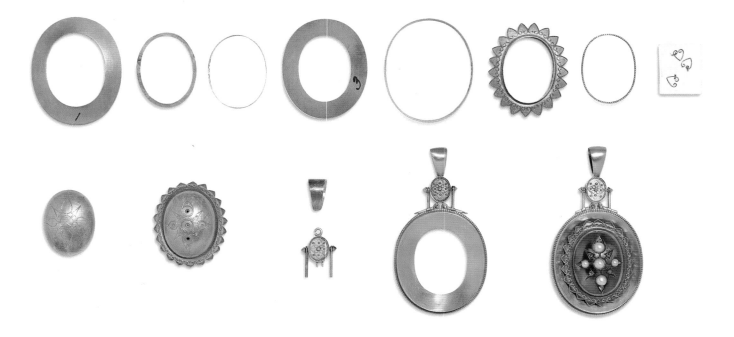

Below: Gold locket decorated with Indian motifs in cloisonné enamel, made by Alexis Falize, *c.*1870. It was shown by Falize at the International Exhibition, London, in 1871, from where it was purchased by the Museum (height 5.3cm/ 2.1in).

Enamelled gold bracelet with locket pendants, set with pearls and diamonds. The cross, anchor and heart represent the Christian virtues of Faith, Hope and Love. It was made *c.*1860 for mourning use (diameter 6.8cm/2.7in).

Opposite: The component parts of a handmade locket, made by the Birmingham manufacturer T. & J. Bragg in 1875, of gold, pearls and diamonds. Top row (*from left to right*): the back, cut from sheet-gold and hammered into shape; two rims for the back compartment; the cupped front; the outer rim; the frill ornament, made by filing out the shape and then soldering; a beaded wire rim that sits within the frill; details of the wire filigree decoration. Bottom row (*from left to right*): the embossed centre panel with the pattern outlined by the engraver; the frill added to the embossed centre; the loop and the ornament below; the finished frame; the completed pendant.

Below: Gold locket of 1871 decorated with a Gothic letter 'L' in diamonds. The back is inscribed 'In remembrance of L.B.F. Oct 7th 1871, from C.G.S.F.' Inside is a photograph of the woman it commemorates (who is also wearing a locket) and a strand of her hair (height 5.4cm/2.1in).

NOVELTIES

The Victorian fondness for small humorous trinkets, known as 'novelties', emerged in the late 1860s and continued into the new century. A huge variety of subjects were used over these years, as manufacturers responded imaginatively to the constant demand for new and different ideas. Amongst the more eccentric designs were earrings shaped as cauldrons, omnibuses, windmills and watering cans.

Sporting novelties, including miniature tennis racquets (often with a pearl ball), golf clubs, fishing tackle and oars, and animal pins, of pigs, bears, poodles and donkeys, were the most popular. The majority of these pieces were small, mass-produced and inexpensive. There was a constant market for hunting themes, which were worn by both sexes: in *Mr Sponge's Sporting Tour* (1852) the author R. S. Surtees alludes to men wearing 'story-telling buttons – a fox with TALLY-HO or a fox's head grinning in grim death'. Pins decorated with foxes and hunting horns were still a flourishing line in 1901 when the Goldsmiths & Silversmiths Company offered ones topped with running or crouching foxes at a little over £1 and diamond fox heads with ruby eyes for up to £27. More unusually, hunting trophies such as deer teeth, grouse claws and, in India (where they were traditionally believed to ward off evil), tiger claws were mounted in jewellery from the 1840s onwards. The vivid plumage and metallic iridescence of exotic birds and insects was used to create colourful jewellery and dress trimmings akin to taxidermy. Two firms exhibited such pieces at the London Exhibition of 1872, using humming birds and beetles from South America, which were mounted on base metal fittings.

Perhaps the most ingenious novelties were the moving jewels powered by electricity, which were first seen at the Paris Exhibition of 1867 and included a skull, a rabbit playing a drum, and birds and butterflies with fluttering wings. They were designed to be worn as cravat pins or on the bodice or in the hair and were connected to a miniature Voltaic battery concealed in the wearer's pocket. Toys of such sophistication as these were not made in great quantities.

Right: 'Blue creeper' feather earrings, with glass eyes and base-metal mounts, probably exhibited at the London Exhibition of 1872. Their beaks point upward to metal flies, while the fringed detail around their base is a typical feature of *c.*1870 (height 9cm/3.5in).

Below: Earrings of gilt metal set with iridescent Brazilian Tortoise Leaf beetles, *c.*1860 (height 4cm/1.6in).

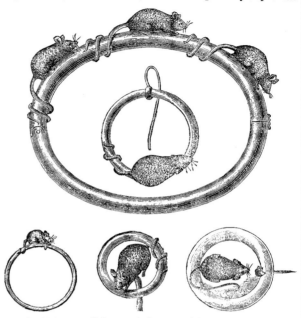

MESSRS THORNHILL'S MOUSE JEWELLERY.

ECCENTRIC jewellery, to serve the caprice of the day, has run through many phases and shapes of late. Chinese and Japanese designs, beetles, butterflies, and spiders have all had their turn, and snake bangles must have been sold by tens of thousands. But the newest thing in this line is the mouse jewellery, brought out in registered designs by Messrs Thornhill and Co., of New Bond-street. However disagreeable a live mouse may be running about one's room, in itself it is a gracefully shaped little

animal, which may well form part of an eccentric ornament, especially if skilfully modelled and arranged. Whether the substitution of little pigs in the place of mice, which Messrs Thornhill likewise intend to introduce, and which are now the fashion in Paris, will turn out equally satisfactory from an artistic point of view, remains to be seen.

Above: French stick pin of enamelled gold and diamonds, c.1867. The gold bone at the neck serves as an electrical terminal, and when connected to a battery the diamond eyes roll and the jaws snap (height 9.2cm/3.6in).

Above right: Engraving from *Queen* magazine, 31 July 1880.

Right: Brooch with a reverse-intaglio crystal of a Yorkshire Terrier, c.1875–90 (diameter 2cm/0.79in). The three-dimensional effect is achieved by engraving and painting on the flat back of a domed piece of crystal. An English invention, it was first shown by Lambert & Rawlings at the London Exhibition of 1862.

NINETEENTH-CENTURY MACHINE-MADE JEWELLERY

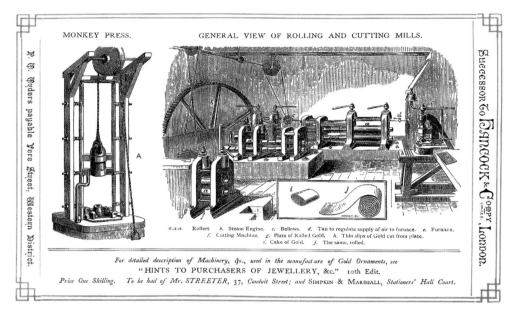

MONKEY PRESS.   GENERAL VIEW OF ROLLING AND CUTTING MILLS.

a.a.a. Rollers   b. Steam Engine.   c. Bellows.   d. Tap to regulate supply of air to furnace.   e. Furnace.
f. Cutting Machine.   g. Plate of Rolled Gold.   h. Thin slips of Gold cut from plate.
i. Cake of Gold.   j. The same, rolled.

For detailed description of Machinery, &c., used in the manufacture of Gold Ornaments, see
"HINTS TO PURCHASERS OF JEWELLERY, &c." 10th Edit.
Price One Shilling.   To be had of Mr. STREETER, 37, Conduit Street; and SIMPKIN & MARSHALL, Stationers' Hall Court.

Machinery used in the jewellery trade, illustrated in Edwin Streeter's catalogue, c.1870. Streeter explained in 1867 how 'the gold, instead of being hammered into the required thickness, is passed through the steam Rolling Machine and can be pressed out to any extent in a few minutes. It is then, with the greatest rapidity, cut into [the required shape] by the Cutting Press.' The Monkey Press created form and pattern in a single action, when the gold sheet was pressed between the steel die and its matching lead impression inside the heavy drop hammer.

By the 1860s the jewellery trade had been transformed by mechanization. The traditional methods of creating delicate forms and patterns out of solid blocks of metal – modelling, casting, embossing, chasing and engraving – continued to be carried out by hand at the most exclusive end of the market. But new machinery and the use of gold-plated base metal enabled similar effects to be achieved by ingenious short cuts, resulting in the mass production of large quantities of cheaper jewellery.

One of the most vociferous advocates of machine-production using precious metals was the London jeweller Edwin Streeter. In his book *Hints to Purchasers of Jewellery* (1867) he detailed the six days of skilled work necessary to make a gold bracelet by hand and compared this with the two days required when most of the work was done by machine. He concluded that, for the jeweller, 'the more quickly he can manufacture such articles, the cheaper he can sell them; getting for himself a fair profit, and giving to the public advantages which they could not have had under the old system'. The difference in the price of the finished pieces was substantial: his machine-made gold earrings cost £1.10s. in contrast with those made by hand, which were priced between £3 and £5.

Much of the required technology had been developed during the Industrial Revolution: the manufacturers of Sheffield plate in the late eighteenth century had developed machines for rolling out sheets of a uniform thickness and had also perfected the hardening of steel to the degree needed to make strong, lasting dies. Chainmaking – which by hand was extremely laborious – was a later development, following inventions in the production of industrial-steel chains. The first chainmaking machines appeared in the 1850s, with improvements and new varieties giving rise to many patents during the 1860s. The setting of gemstones continued to require hand work, but great economies were achieved with the development of mass-produced collets stamped out of metal sheet. Prefabricated collets were shown at the London Exhibition of 1862 by the Parisian firm Bouret & Ferré, and it was estimated that they represented a saving in terms of metal and time of between 60 and 80 percent.

Such innovations, while being rapidly adopted by manufacturers throughout Europe and America, did not gain universal approval. In her book *The Art of Beauty* (1878) Mrs Haweis complained that 'Machine-made jewellery has debased to the utmost the few fine forms which once were popular, and increased the ignorant and mistaken craze for "sets" and "pairs"... It is food for regret that it has been found possible to manufacture so much cheap work, and to find buyers among the vulgar and uncultured masses.' Gentler regrets were expressed for the loss of individuality and spontaneity that mass production had brought, and it certainly fostered in many a greater regard for artistic designs and traditional crafts. However, nothing could turn back the tide or dispel the great popular appeal of affordable jewellery for all classes.

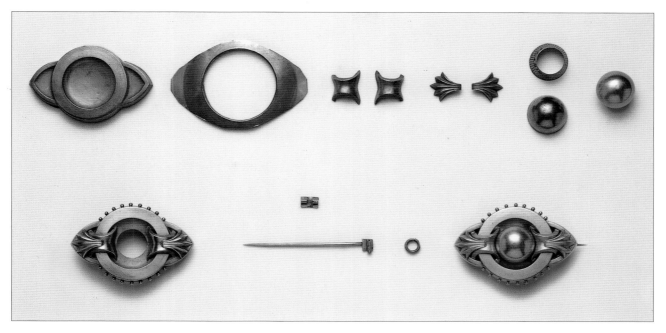

Demonstration model of a machine-made gold brooch with its component parts, made by T. & J. Bragg of Birmingham in 1875. Birmingham was the centre of mechanized jewellery production in Britain.

Steel dies used to stamp out the parts of the gold brooch above. The patterns were chiselled out by die-sinkers – who needed both technical skill and artistic ability – before the steel was hardened.

JET AND VICTORIAN MOURNING

A hand-coloured albumen print of Elizabeth Howard, the widow of a Lancashire cotton manufacturer, who died in 1869. Still in full mourning, her black jewellery comprises two strings of jet beads that hang from a brooch at her neck and long pendent earrings.

Nobody requires to be told that a superabundance of jewellery is in especially bad taste at seasons of mourning. A few trinkets, however, must be worn, if only to accentuate the general sombreness of the costume.
QUEEN MAGAZINE, 23 JANUARY 1892

During Queen Victoria's reign it was customary for a widow to wear full mourning dress – usually black crape – for a year and a day after her husband's death. This was followed by at least nine months of half-mourning, when a more lustrous black fabric might be allowed, perhaps trimmed with black braid or with a white collar and cuffs. Black was also worn to mark the demise of great public figures such as the Duke of Wellington in 1852 and Prince Albert in 1861. The wearing of jewellery was equally restricted, and jet – which could be intricately carved, left matt black or polished to a lustrous sheen – was one of the few acceptable adornments.

Jet is a black fossilized wood, and one of the richest sources of it is near Whitby on the Yorkshire coast. This town therefore became the centre of an extensive small-scale industry employing at its height in the early 1870s between 1200 and 1500 men, women and children. Workshops varied in size from large businesses like that of Charles Bryan, who exhibited at the Paris Exhibition of 1862 and who had offices in Birmingham and London, to small attic studios. The town achieved an international reputation, exporting to Europe, British colonies and the United States of America.

Beads, both plain and faceted, were an important part of production, as were jet chains, which were made by splitting and re-gluing alternate links. Larger pieces had more decorative potential, although designs seldom reached beyond popular stereotypes: vines, ferns and lilies of the valley were carefully copied from nature, while Christian symbols, notably crosses and anchors, were also favourite motifs. Design education was attempted with the establishment of drawing classes for Whitby craftsmen in the 1850s. However, the *Whitby Times* recorded that when the pioneering designer Christopher Dresser visited in 1874 to distribute prizes amongst the jet workers, he was impressed by their skill but not by their artistic sensitivity, and he recommended that they adopt simpler, more individual designs.

Although jet was much cheaper than enamelled-gold mourning jewellery, it remained sufficiently costly for there to be a flourishing trade in substitutes. Jet waste could be recycled and combined with rubber to make a mouldable compound, while from the 1860s the French were using *bois durci* – a composition of hardwood sawdust, blood and albumen mixed with binding and colouring agents. With both materials production costs were minimized as complex designs were moulded rather than carved by hand. The same was true with vulcanite, an early plastic made by heating India rubber and sulphur, which was in widespread use by the 1870s. Natural alternatives included stained horn, which was softened in boiling water, then pressed between hot dies, and Irish bog-oak. In addition black-glass ornaments, known as French jet, were produced in many parts of Europe. The workshops of Whitby were greatly affected by these products and complained vigorously whenever they found goods wrongly marketed as 'Whitby jet'.

Left: In 1869 a new sophistication was noted by the curator of the Whitby Museum, who wrote to the *Art Journal* that now, the 'best workmen are imitating the beautiful Roman cameos, and models of antique gems'. This parure of 1870–85 is carved with female heads, which symbolize Night, framed by foliage, flowers and scrolls (height of the earrings 6.5cm/2.5in).

Below: This cross of roses linked with a ribbon bow is of moulded vulcanite and dates from *c.*1875 (height 8.2cm/3.2in). The colour of this manmade alternative has not proved very durable – on prolonged exposure to light vulcanite turns brown

ART NOUVEAU IN PARIS AND BRUSSELS

Art Nouveau, a style distinguished by its sinuous curves and intense sensitivity to nature, was at its height in Paris and Brussels during the years around 1900. It pervaded all the decorative arts and took its name from Samuel Bing's shop, La Maison de l'Art Nouveau, which had opened in Paris in 1895.

In jewellery it brought a new emphasis, away from symmetrical arrangements of valuable gemstones to more painterly compositions, where lesser stones were preferred for their colours and placed in finely sculpted gold settings enhanced with toning shades of enamel. Nature was the principal source of inspiration for these jewellers, but their approach owed much to Japanese art and oriental ideas of beauty. Although often seen as a period of softened and romanticized naturalism, beneath Art Nouveau lay a *fin-de-siècle* decadence and the sinister preoccupations of the Symbolist painters. Among the blossom-heavy branches and flowing strands of golden hair there sometimes lurked a preoccupation with nature's cruelty and with death.

It was the Parisian jeweller René Lalique who first applied the language of Art Nouveau to jewellery, and his work was crucial in defining and promoting this new style between 1895 and 1900. Georges Fouquet showed his first Art Nouveau pieces, including an orchid designed by Charles Desrosiers in 1898, and the following year began a collaboration with the poster artist Alphonse Mucha. Together they created complex ornaments of plaques linked by decorated chains, similar to the painted jewels on his posters, and in 1901 Mucha went on to transform Fouquet's shop into one of the most sumptuous Art Nouveau interiors in Paris (see page 145). At the Paris Exhibition of 1900, which championed the Art Nouveau style, René Lalique, Maison Vever and Lucien Gaillard were each awarded a Grand Prix for their Art Nouveau jewellery, with Fouquet and Eugène Feuillâtre winning gold medals. The other great exponent of the Art Nouveau style was Belgian jeweller and sculptor Philippe Wolfers, who was singled out as Lalique's equal by many of their contemporaries. Drawing on a similar range of themes and techniques he created a magnificent series of unique jewels between the mid-1890s and 1905.

The V&A acquired its first Art Nouveau jewellery in 1901 directly from the Salon de la Société des Artistes Français in Paris. Several pieces were bought, including Fouquet's hornet brooch opposite, which cost about £75. The then Director of the Museum commented on their relevance to art and design students 'as illustrating modern techniques in adapting various materials to new developments of ornamental design'.

Top left: A stem of mistletoe with green-enamel leaves and pearl berries curves across a gold relief of three female heads in this brooch by Fouquet, c.1900. It is framed by a slender line of diamonds (height 2.3cm/ 0.91in).

Centre left: The central plaque from a dog-collar necklace, c.1900. Within its undulating gold frame is a branch of wisteria with enamelled and diamond-set blooms, and *plique à jour*, or unbacked enamel, enamel leaves (height 4.7cm/1.9in). Wisteria frequently occurs in Japanese prints and was a popular motif in Art Nouveau jewellery.

Right: An orchid jewel of gold, *plique à jour* enamel, rubies and diamonds, to be worn in the hair. Designed and made by Wolfers c.1900. The light flooding through the upper petal demonstrates the luminous beauty of transparent enamel (height 7.6cm/3in).

Bottom left: Brooch of a hornet hovering below an open flower. The wings and petals are of *plique à jour*, while the more solid stem, swirling into the distance, is of translucent enamel on chased gold. It was designed by Desrosiers and made by Fouquet c.1901 (height 6.2cm/2.5in).

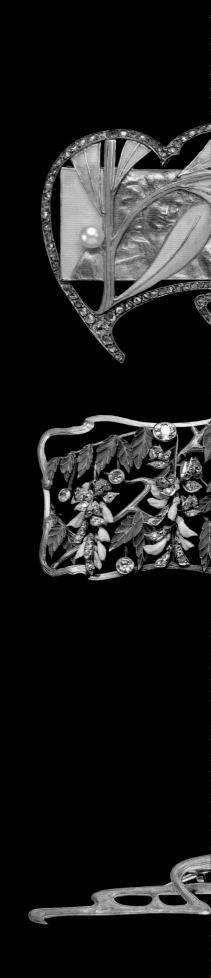

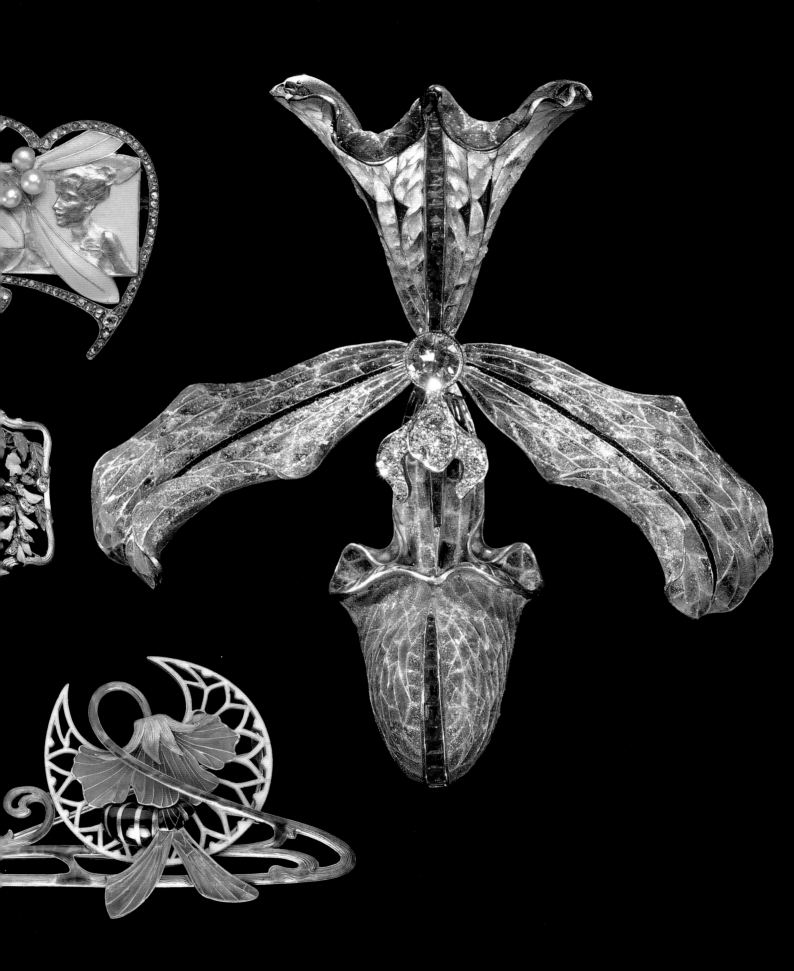

THE JEWELLERY OF RENÉ LALIQUE, 1860–1945

On his visit to the Paris Exhibition in 1900, the journalist from the *Jeweller and Metalworker* commented: 'The eye is soon attracted by one large exhibit continually encompassed by crowds of admirers. It is the exhibit of René Lalique, the admitted king of Paris fashions.' Lalique's work, with its diversity of subject matter and its harmonies of colour and form, entranced and amazed those who saw it. His innovative style, which had been heralded as transforming jewellery in France from an industry to an art at the Paris Salon of 1895, now brought him universal triumph.

Lalique had undergone a conventional apprenticeship aged 16 with Parisian jeweller Louis Aucoc, followed by two years in England at the art school attached to the Crystal Palace in Sydenham. During the 1880s he had designed for various of the leading Paris jewellers, often inspired by nature but working within the diamond-set conventions of the time. However, during the 1890s, after an exhausting programme of technical research into enamel and glass, he created what was to be a new vocabulary of materials and a new aesthetic style. The work he exhibited in 1897 included fragile enamelled flowers and jewelled horn combs. It was a radical departure from what his contemporaries were doing and was heralded as a new style that would rejuvenate the world of jewellery.

Nature was the principal source of Lalique's inspiration. He drew not only on the conventionally appealing, such as sweet peas, pansies and butterflies, but also on unlikely subjects like sycamore seeds, grass-hoppers and even serpents and wasps. His imagery reflected nature's cycles – all seasons are represented, as are the stages from birth

to death and decay. He delighted also in the human form, creating figurative jewellery of exquisite sensuality, with reliefs of female figures or of embracing lovers. A love of Japanese art encouraged a simplicity and asymmetry in his work and underlay his talent for capturing the essence of a subject without labouring over its detailed physical characteristics.

Lalique convinced his public that value resided in aesthetic effect and technical virtuosity, rather than the traditional currency of precious stones. He chose his materials on this basis, and amongst his most distinctive innovations were the use of horn, which he bleached, moulded and carved; and glass, which could be given any colour and cast in finely carved moulds. Although he did use diamonds, they were seldom prominent in a design. Opal, with its mysterious flashes of colour, was one of his favourite stones, and he captured a similar effect with frosted and enamelled glass.

After the First World War Lalique turned entirely to glass, although this did include some elements for use in jewellery. Typical of these were beads shaped as flower heads or leaves that were threaded on silk cords, and moulded plaques that were mounted as brooches. Lalique's most notable patrons were the collector Calouste Gulbenkian, who, from 1895, commissioned almost 150 pieces of jewellery and glass, and Sarah Bernhardt, who wore his jewellery both on and off the stage.

Above: Design for a pendant of a woman's head framed with the intertwined flowers and foliage of water lilies. This was illustrated in the *Magazine of Art* in 1902, a time when Lalique's work was not widely known in London.

Right: A brooch of cast glass designed by Lalique, *c.*1920. The glass plaque is colourless, its pink glow coming from the metal foil set behind it. Traces of a contrasting blue pigment remain on the surface. The three grasshoppers reflect Lalique's enduring fascination with insects (diameter 4.5cm/1.8in).

Opposite: Tiara comb and bodice ornament, *c.*1903–4. The frame work of the tiara is of horn, the petals of the sweet-pea flowers are of glass, the stems and leaves are of enamelled gold and the gemstones are topaz (width of tiara 15.9cm/6.3in).

C. R. ASHBEE AND THE GUILD OF HANDICRAFT

Among pioneers of the artistic jewellery movement, Mr. C. R. Ashbee holds an honourable place. He stood almost alone at the beginning, when he first made known the jewellery designed by him, and produced under his personal direction by the Guild and School of Handicraft in the East End. It was immediately apparent that here was no tentative nor half-hearted caprice, but that a genuine and earnest phase of an ancient craft had been re-established.
AYMER VALLANCE, 'MODERN JEWELLERY AND FANS',
THE STUDIO, SPECIAL WINTER NUMBER, 1901–2

The Guild of Handicraft was founded by Ashbee in 1888. As both a workshop and a school, it was dedicated to promoting traditional craft skills, and its foundation was a philanthropic response to the lack of satisfying employment in London's East End. The Guild concentrated initially on woodcarving and metalworking, but in 1891 classes in the more delicate skills of jewellery were introduced, and its first jewellery was exhibited in 1893. As Ashbee intended, this early work, produced by self-taught craftsmen, was startlingly different from the commercially produced jewellery of the day. It was mostly

Left: Advertisement from the *British Architect* of December 1903, showing the wide range of the Guild's production. In the Museum's collection are two pieces that relate closely to the central necklace – a turquoise-set silver-wire circlet and a rectangular brooch of a ship like the central plaque.

Opposite
Top left: Pendant of a ship, of enamelled gold, silver, opal, diamond sparks and tourmalines. Designed by Ashbee and made by the Guild c.1903 (height 7cm/2.8in). The opal is from

Australia, where they had been discovered in 1889.

Bottom left: An early brooch of enamelled copper, decorated with silver wire, blister pearls and three irregular pearl drops. Designed by Ashbee and made by the Guild, c.1896 (diameter 7.2cm/2.8in).

Right: Peacock pendant of silver and gold set with diamond sparks and blister pearls, with a demantoid garnet for the eye. Designed by Ashbee and made by the Guild in 1901 (height of pendant 10.2cm/4in).

made of silver, often decorated with loosely naturalistic spiralling or wavelike forms, and was distinguished by its large size and unashamed lack of refinement.

In the years around 1900 the workshop expanded to include several more conventionally trained craftsmen, and the jewellery became more elaborate. Vivid effects were achieved in different coloured stones and rich enamels, while frequent use was made of what Ashbee described as 'the long, grey, unfinished pear-shaped pearls, so favourite a stone through the Middle Ages and the Renaissance'. Ashbee's admiration of the Renaissance was also apparent in his love of pendants. The peacock, a symbol of both pride and the Resurrection, was one of his favourite motifs; the other was a galleon, which, as a pun on the Guild's name, was known as the 'Craft of the Guild'.

In the late 1890s Ashbee began translating the sixteenth-century goldsmith Benvenuto Cellini's *Treatises* on goldsmithing and sculpture, which, dedicated to the Guild's metalworkers, was published 1898. Through it he hoped to understand the practical techniques used by pre-industrial craftsmen and to be able to introduce these into his workshops. He also wanted his craftsmen to be inspired by surviving examples of historic metalwork and created a small gallery where he arranged exhibitions of work borrowed from the V&A – in its previous incarnation of the South Kensington Museum – featuring examples of traditional European folk jewellery.

For most of the 1890s the Guild was based at Essex House on Commercial Road in the East End of London, but in 1902 it moved out to the more wholesome environment of Chipping Campden in the Cotswolds. Sadly this was to mark the beginning of its commercial decline, and the Guild closed in 1908.

THE ART OF ENAMELLING, *CIRCA* 1900

Above: The Wagner Girdle, designed and made by Alexander Fisher for Mrs Emslie J. Horniman between 1893 and 1896, of steel set with paste stones and enamel plaques. The enamels show scenes from

Wagner's operas: (*from left to right*) the death of Tristan, Lohengrin, Siegmund and Siegelinde, the Rhine Maidens, Fafrir, Tannhauser, Tristan and Isolde with the love potion (height 9.7cm/3.8in).

Opposite left: A pendant by Phoebe Traquair entitled *Cupid the Earth Upholder*, dated 1902. It is made of gold and painted enamel; the iridescent 'stones' of coloured and foiled glass (height 7.5cm/3in)

Opposite right: Pendant set with an enamelled plaque of tradescantia and hung with an irregular opal and two amethysts. Made by Nelson and Edith Dawson, 1900, the enamelwork probably done by Edith, who was a keen botanist (height 12.5cm/4.9in).

All the bewildering surfaces, all the depths and lovelinesses that lie darkly in the waters of sea-caves, all the glistening lustre of gleaming gold or silver back and fin of fish, the velvet of the purple sea anemone, the jewelled brilliance of sunshine on snow ... indeed, the very embodiments in colour of the intensity of beauty – these are at hand waiting for expression in enamel.
ALEXANDER FISHER, *THE STUDIO* (1903)

In this lyrical passage enameller and teacher Alexander Fisher championed the supremacy of enamel, praising its unparalleled versatility in colour, opacity and texture. His speciality was painted enamel; descended from the Limoges enamels of the Renaissance, which combined individual artistic vision with a complex and exacting technique. Fisher believed that this painterly method was best suited to 'the embodiment of thoughts, ideas, imaginings, and for those parts of a world which exist only in our minds', but it was used with equal success for subtle depictions of nature, sensitive portraits and figurative scenes.

Fisher's revival of this type of enamelling was initially inspired by lectures given in London in the mid-1880s by Louis Dalpeyrat of Sèvres. He subsequently gained a scholarship to study enamelling in Paris, where he experimented using layers of different translucent colours, highlighted with glinting strips of metal foil beneath the surface. Back in London his work became known through the Arts & Crafts Exhibition Society with whom he regularly showed. It was his teaching, though, that was to have the greatest influence on his contemporaries – from 1896 to 1898 at the Central School of Arts and Crafts, and from 1904 at his own school in Kensington. Although he protested that only by demonstrating the technique could its complexities be explained, he also wrote a series of instructive articles for *The Studio*, which were published as *The Art of Enamelling on Metals* in 1906. This had a considerable impact, and as well as being adopted by professional craftsmen, enamel painting became a popular pastime amongst the upper and middle classes.

Nelson Dawson had attended Fisher's classes and then passed on what he had learnt to his wife Edith, who was a skilled watercolourist and who went on to do most of the enamelling in their joint work. Their first jewellery was shown in 1899 and was set with the subtle botanical studies that were to become so typical of their work. Phoebe Traquair was an Edinburgh artist whose abilities encompassed embroidery, murals and illuminated manuscripts as well as painted enamels. Again she owed her training to Fisher, albeit indirectly, as she was taught by his pupil Lady Gibson Carmichael in 1901. Over the next ten years she created vivid foiled enamel scenes, usually of mythical or spiritual subjects.

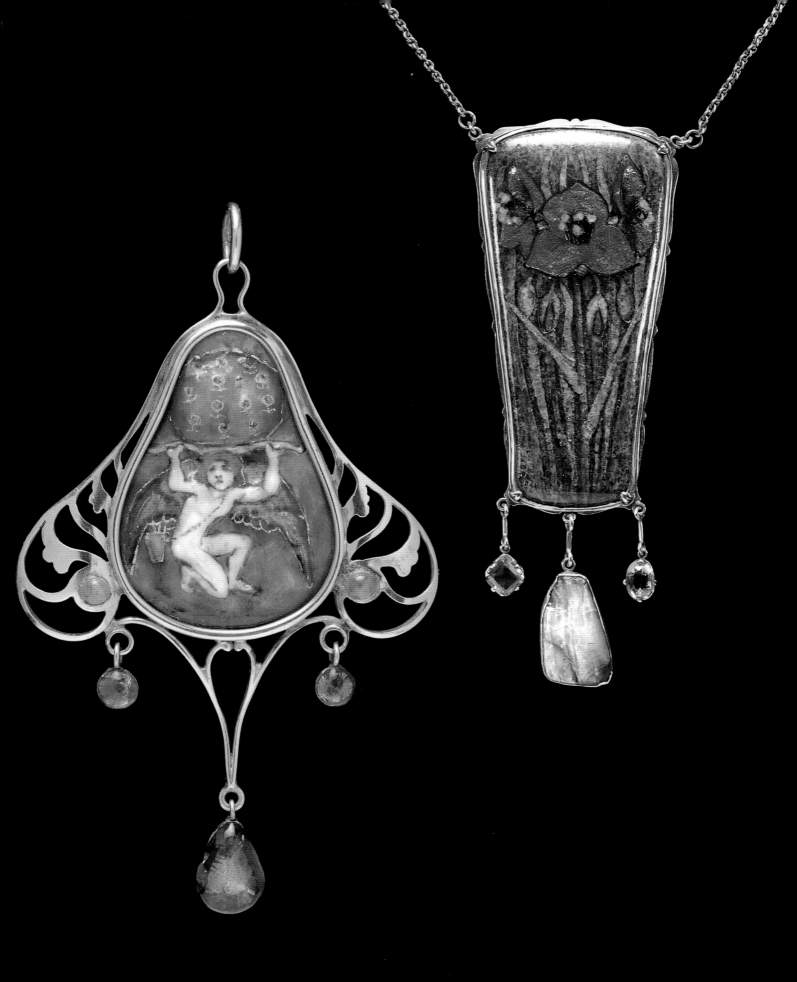

MAY MORRIS'S JEWELLERY

Gold ring in the form of a turret, set with a cabochon ruby dome, 1899–1903. Historicist in feel and influenced by traditional Jewish marriage rings, it was designed by Charles Ricketts.

Left: Jewellery that had formerly belonged to Janey Morris, including a long gold chain, c.1835, on which is threaded her wedding ring, and a citrine brooch, c.1825. The gold bracelet with dragon heads, and the paste-set heart brooch were from Rossetti's collection (height of heart-shaped brooch 3.5 cm/1.4in).

Right: Ivory comb with mother-of-pearl, sapphires, green-stained chalcedony and a fire opal matrix all set in silver. Made by Joseph Hodel of the Bromsgrove Guild c.1906 (height 10.8cm/4.3in)

Silver girdle set with river pearls, garnets and chrysoprase, designed and made by May Morris, 1906.

The pins – one set with milky opal, pearls and topazes, the other with agate, emeralds and pearls – and the heart-shaped pendant set with amazonite, turquoise, pearls and lapis lazuli are also believed to be by May Morris, c. 1903 (height of pendant 5.1cm/2in).

May Morris, the younger daughter of William Morris and his wife Janey, was born in 1862. An important figure in the Arts and Crafts Movement, she is remembered primarily for her skills as an embroideress but was also a talented jeweller. On her death in 1938 she bequeathed to the Museum some of her personal jewellery, and this was added to soon afterwards by her friend and companion Vivien Lobb. Like the contents of most jewellery boxes, the collection is a varied assortment. Some were inherited from her mother, some were designed and made by May herself, and others came from contemporary jewellers.

The pieces that had been Janey Morris's suggest that Janey had a liking for the rich *cannetille* work and textured gold of the 1820s and 1830s. However, the most interesting and unusual pieces were those that her mother had acquired from the painter Dante Gabriel Rossetti, who had been in love with her and had painted her often. During the 1860s Rossetti had frequented the curiosity shops around Leicester Square and Hammersmith, collecting exotic jewellery and accessories for his paintings. The gold dragon bracelet appears on the wrist of the bride in *The Beloved*, painted 1865–6, while the silver heart set with green and pink pastes is worn by Fanny Cornforth as a pendant in *The Blue Bower* of 1865.

May Morris started to design jewellery around the turn of the century, no doubt influenced by Birmingham jewellers Arthur and Georgie Gaskin, who were old family friends. Typical of the Arts and Crafts, she worked with a colourful palette of semi-precious stones. Her heart-shaped pendant was doubtless inspired by the cruder paste-set brooch that had been Rossetti's, and she drew also on the forms and motifs of European folk jewellery. Her silver girdle was exhibited at the Arts & Crafts Exhibition of 1906 and illustrated in the review of it in *The Studio* magazine. At the same exhibition May Morris must have seen and purchased the comb by Josef Hodel of the Bromsgrove Guild. Her ring was from a design by the artist Charles Ricketts, who also created various embroidery designs for her. The little jewellery that he designed tended to be for specific friends and was usually made up by London jeweller Carlo Giuliano.

LIBERTY'S CYMRIC JEWELLERY

Messrs Liberty are indefatigable in supplying increasingly fresh attractions without giving frail woman a chance to pause and consider her resources. Once inside those tempting portals away fly all economical scruples. We cannot resist this, and our very souls crave that, and, above all for the immediate moment, must we own some specimen of the Cymric gold and silver jewellery.
QUEEN MAGAZINE, 27 SEPTEMBER 1902

The Cymric range of jewellery and silver, advertised as 'a characteristically original and artistic departure in silver-craft', was launched in May 1899 by Arthur Lasenby Liberty and his director John Llewellyn – whose Welsh ancestry probably inspired its name. A total of 19 pieces of jewellery appeared in this first collection – mostly waist clasps and brooches – but this was soon extended to include pendants, necklaces, rings, hatpins, sleeve links and buttons. It was to prove an extremely successful and long-lived venture, producing distinctive, elegant and reasonably priced jewellery until 1927.

Although it shared many of the typical features of Arts and Crafts jewellery – such as cabochon stones, enamelled or hammer-beaten surfaces, and the use of silver – its production was commercially rather than idealistically motivated. Cheaper machine processes were used whenever possible, even to the extent of incorporating 'hand-beaten' hammer-marks on the steel dies that stamped out the pieces, with only the most intricate work being done by hand. Thus, to Ashbee's exasperation, Liberty's were able to achieve a similar effect for a fraction of the cost of work that was completely made by hand. With the exception of the earliest pieces, the jewellery was manufactured by W. H. Haseler of Birmingham

Liberty's were keen to present the Cymric range as a single entity and at no point identified the different hands of the many designers who contributed to it. If pieces were entered for Arts and Crafts Society exhibitions the designers had to be credited, but otherwise work remained anonymous. They were an exceptionally innovative and talented team. Birmingham provided some of them, notably the painter Oliver Baker, whose distinctive entwined strapwork patterns are reminiscent of Renaissance ironwork, Arthur and Georgie Gaskin and Bernard Cuzner. In London Rex Silver, the head of the Silver Studios in Hammersmith, became the principal

Top: Silver and enamel buckle of 1903, probably designed by Jessie M. King (height 4.8 cm/1.9in).

Above: A waist clasp of silver set with an opal, probably designed by Oliver Baker, c.1899, and made by Haseler's of Birmingham. This particular clasp belonged to John Llewellyn's wife. The same model but set with a turquoise matrix would have cost £2.5s. in 1900 (height 10.8cm/4.3in).

source of designs for Liberty's. Some of the most exceptional designs, particularly those based on Celtic interlace, can be attributed to Archibald Knox, the Manx designer and teacher, who worked for the Silver Studios from 1898.

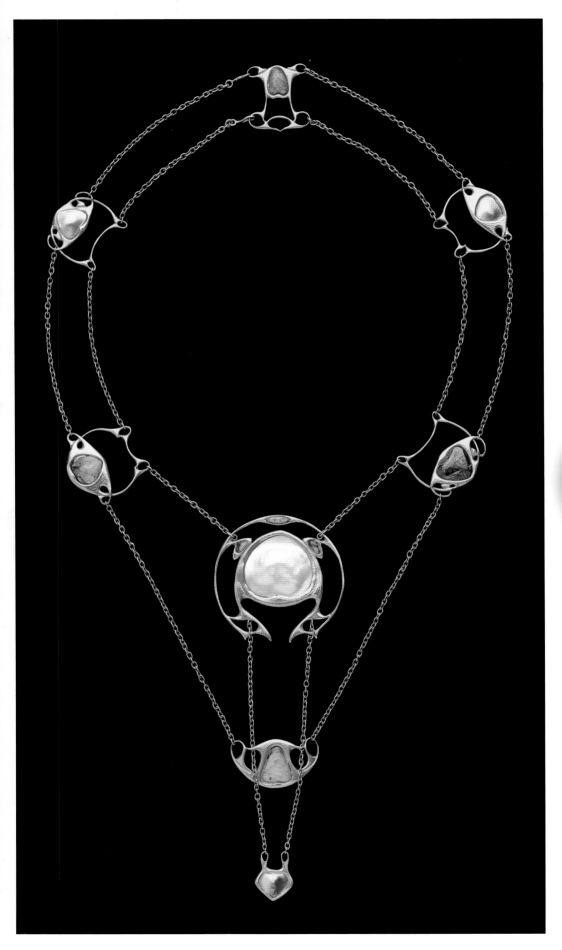

Necklace of gold, blister pearls and opals designed by Archibald Knox for Liberty's, c.1902, and made by Haseler's of Birmingham (fastened length 24 cm/9.4in).

Silver and enamel button, embossed with a line of trees. Made by Haseler's of Birmingham in 1905, it would have cost in the region of 5 shillings (diameter 3cm/1.2in).

HENRY WILSON AND THE GASKINS

Opposite top:Winged tiara of rock crystal, chalcedony, gold and enamel, in the centre an oxidized silver figure of Cupid in a shell. Designed by Henry Wilson, c.1908 (width 21.2cm/8.3in).

Bottom left: 'Love-in-a-Mist' necklace of enamelled silver set with pearls. Designed by Georgie Gaskin and made in the Gaskins' workshop, c.1910, for Mrs Emmeline Cadbury (length of roundel and pendant 8.5cm/3.3in).

Bottom right: Pendant of enamelled gold, cabochon sapphires and pearls designed by Henry Wilson, c.1914. Here it is attached to a seed-pearl necklace, but it may also be worn, with a matching roundel, as a cloak clasp (diameter of pendant 4.8cm/1.9in).

Below: Design drawing by Wilson for the pendant.

enry Wilson trained originally as an architect, and his time as chief assistant to Arts and Crafts architect J. D. Sedding undoubtedly fostered his love of medieval ornament and the sculptural quality later apparent in his work in metals. He first turned his attention to metalwork in the early 1890s and by 1896 was teaching at the Central School of Arts and Crafts in London. By 1901 he was on the staff at the Royal College of Art, and in 1903 he published his excellent manual *Silverwork and Jewellery*. In its preface he advised the student to 'feed his imagination on old work', encouraging an historicism that is evident in his own designs. Other distinctive features of his jewels are their skilful modelling and intricate three-dimensional construction, their unusual and subtly coloured stones, and their superb vibrant enamelling. Wilson employed talented craftsmen in his workshop, including several Italians. Amongst those who trained with him were John Paul Cooper and H. G. Murphy, both of whom went on to successful independent careers in metalwork and jewellery.

Husband and wife Arthur and Georgie Gaskin had both been students at Birmingham School of Art. They began to make jewellery in 1899 and were immediately applauded in Arts and Crafts circles for providing an artistic, handmade counterbalance to what *The Studio Special Number* of 1901–2 described as the 'large amount of very deplorable jewellery' produced by Birmingham's jewellery industry. Georgie Gaskin later described how their studio operated: 'In the jewellery I did all the designing & he did all the enamel, and we both executed the work with our assistants.' The bulk of their output consisted of necklaces and pendants, made of twisted wire and densely packed leaves and flowers, reminiscent of traditional French and Flemish folk jewellery. Most pieces were in silver and decorated with enamel and semi-precious stones. *The Studio* approvingly commented that 'Absence of mathematical uniformity ... gives a living and human interest to the work, and a decorative quality which machine-made articles cannot claim to possess.' In 1902 Arthur Gaskin was made head of the Vittoria Street School for Silversmiths and Jewellers in Birmingham, a position he held until 1924.

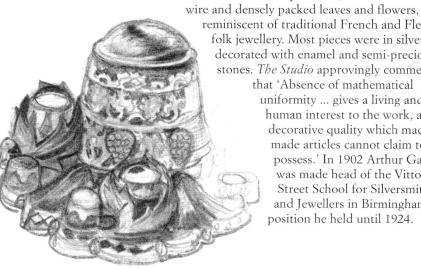

FASHION ACCESSORIES, 1900–1930

Silver and enamel cigarette box made in London in 1903, designed as an envelope that has arrived in the post. Its enamelled postmarks for 23 and (on the back) 24 December indicate that it must have been commissioned as a Christmas gift (width 9.2 cm/3.6in).

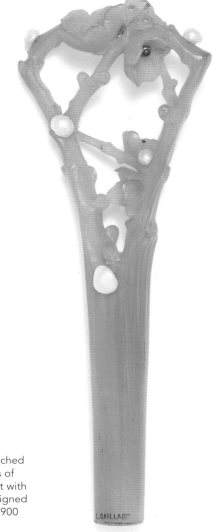

Parasol handle of bleached horn carved as a trellis of twigs and blossom, set with pearls and rubies, designed by Lucien Gaillard, c.1900 (height 14.5cm/5.7in).

Elaborate jewelled items that are not worn but carried for display have always been part of a goldsmith or jeweller's production. In the early years of the century parasols for ladies and fancy-topped canes for gentlemen were important additions to daytime wear, while in the decades that followed the most typical accessories were those connected with smoking and cosmetics, both of which became fashionable for women after the First World War.

Although the greatest impact of the parasol was from its silk fabric and trimmings, jewellers were often called upon to create what the *Queen* magazine in January 1900 described as 'eccentricities in umbrellas and stick handles' and to supply the metal or tortoiseshell covers for the rib-ends. 'Stones of various kinds, malachite, lapis lazuli, cornelian, and jet, are all called into requisition for these. Large balls, set in silver or *repoussé* silver handles are the mode. If an animal or reptile's head is represented, the eyes are gems.' Fabergé's designers came up with amusing hardstone animals, including a frog clinging to the end of the upturned stick and a pair of bears locked in a bear-hug. In Paris Art Nouveau themes were used, and handles were carved from the bleached horn that is more often associated with decorative hair combs. Lucien Gaillard created some extraordinarily beautiful carved hornwork, with asymmetrically arranged blossoms.

During the 1920s smoking accessories – cigarette cases and cigarette holders – were designed in large numbers for women. At the same time the acceptance of women wearing make-up and even applying it in public resulted in luxuriant cosmetic or vanity cases being made by all the major jewellery houses. Some consisted of two matching cases, a cylindrical one for lipstick and a flatter square or rounded one for powder, which were carried by the short chains that linked them together. Alternatively a single box would contain separate compartments for powder, lipstick and a miniature comb. Slightly larger cases, which could also hold cigarettes, were made to replace evening bags. The flat surfaces of all these cases, made of coloured golds, silver, enamel or hardstone, were ideal panels for the geometric and oriental motifs of Art Deco.

Above: Vanity case of jadeite, black onyx and diamonds, with a floral panel of lapis lazuli, turquoise, malachite, rhodochrosite, quartz and mother-of-pearl. Made in Paris, c.1926, for Lacloche Frères and probably sold in their London branch (length 8.3cm/3.3in).

Right: The gold interior of the vanity case, with a mirror inside the lid and two hinged compartments for powder and rouge divided by a detachable lipstick case that springs up as the lid is opened.

Telescopic cigarette holder of stained wood inlaid with silver wire, c.1925 (length 27cm/10.6in).

ART DECO

I n late August 1925 *Vogue* reported that 'The richness of jewels continues in Paris, with diamonds as the solid foundation on which practically everything rests. They are combined with sapphires, with emeralds, with rubies – all the royal family of jewels – in brooches, in bracelets, in necklaces, in earrings.'

Between the First and Second World Wars the commissioning and wearing of opulent jewellery in Society continued on a grand scale but with a radical departure in terms of design. French designer Paul Iribe wrote in 1930 of the need to 'sacrifice the flower on the altar of Cubism and the machine', and although stylized naturalistic ornament did still feature, abstract geometric forms predominated – in response to the simple lines favoured by dress designers and the more dynamic lifestyle enjoyed by wealthier women. Stark motifs were derived from modern architecture or machine parts, while at the same time more exotic effects were inspired by Indian jewellery, Oriental art and Egyptian iconography. Dense concentrations of precious stones, ranked together in geometric patterns and held by the most delicate and discreet platinum or white-gold settings, or vivid blocks of contrasting colours, characterized the jewellery of the 1920s and '30s. This minimal and streamlined style only became known as Art Deco in the 1960s, in recognition of the importance of the Exposition International des Arts Décoratifs et Industriels Modernes in Paris in 1925, which had been dedicated to new and original work.

Boyish hairstyles such as the Eton Crop brought long earrings back into fashion. Necklaces followed suite, often further extended by a matching pendant or jewelled tassel. Many were made of simple geometric links encrusted with precious stones, a pattern that was also often used for bracelets. One of the most distinctive forms of brooch was the double clip, which came apart into two identical halves that could be worn on facing lapels or on opposite sides of a neckline.

Discoveries of new diamond sources in Africa expanded the supply of precious stones. The long, rectangular baguette cut became one of the most fashionable shapes, often juxtaposed with round brilliants to give areas of contrasting pattern and reflection within a uniformly white piece. Black and white jewellery, where glossy black onyx was contrasted with diamonds, was also considered chic – as the French magazine *Fémina* explained in 1926: 'Its sombre sheen makes a paved diamond ground shine out more splendidly, more brightly.' Black onyx is rare in nature but was made from a paler chalcedony by immersing it in a boiling sugar solution for several days then heating it in sulphuric acid to carbonize the sugar.

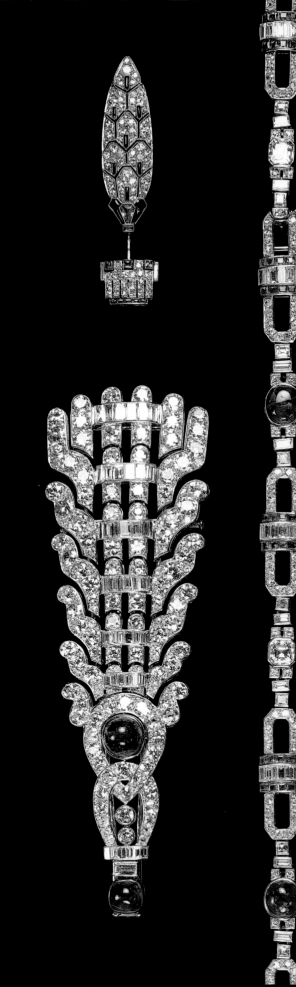

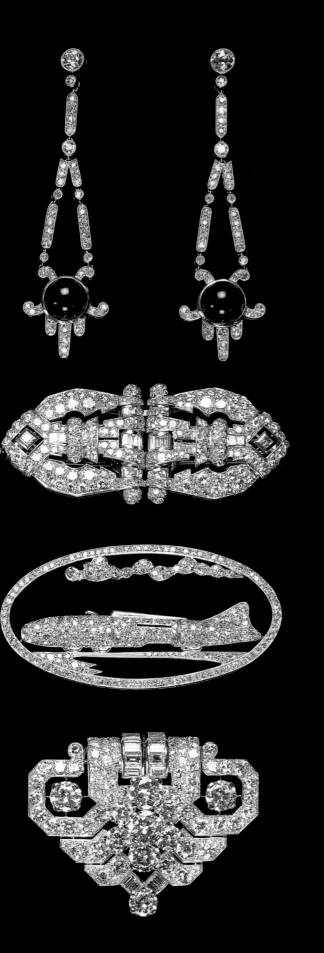

Above: Brooch of lapis lazuli and blue glass set in white gold, designed by Raymond Templier, Paris, c.1934.

Right: Ring of amber, black onyx and jadeite set in platinum and gold, designed by Georges Fouquet, Paris, between 1930 and 1935.

Left: Art Deco jewellery set with brilliant-cut and baguette-cut diamonds, emeralds and black onyx: cypress-tree brooch retailed by Lacloche Frères, c.1927; brooch that when inverted may be worn as a pendant, French, c.1930; necklace that converts into a pair of bracelets, French, c.1930; pair of earrings retailed by Janesich, Paris, c.1925; double clip in platinum, probably English, c.1930; oval brooch commemorating the car 'Thunderbolt', presented to the wife of Captain George Eyston, who broke the World Land Speed Record in it in 1937; brooch made by Cartier, London, in 1940 (height of brooch lower right, 3.9cm/1.5in, the rest to scale).

TWO PROFILES: NAUM SLUTZKY AND ALEXANDER CALDER

Naum Slutzky was born in the Ukraine and studied fine art then engineering in Vienna, before working as a goldsmith at the Wiener Werkstätte. In 1919 he was appointed as a teacher at the Bauhaus in Weimar, in the department of Product Design. Bauhaus principles of applying industrial imagery to domestic areas of design underpinned Slutzky's work as a jeweller and also formed a link with some of the starker motifs of contemporary French Art Deco jewellers. From 1927 he worked as an industrial designer until 1933 when he fled from Nazi Germany. Although he worked in conventional materials such as gold and cabochon stones, he was also fascinated by the newly commercially available chromium-plated brass. Slutzky settled in England where he had a successful and influential career as a teacher in various colleges, including Dartington Hall in Devon, the Royal College of Art and Birmingham's College of Art and Crafts, where he was Head of the School of Industrial Design. Although he made very little jewellery between the mid-1930s and 1960, the early 1960s were again highly productive years, when he worked principally in silver decorated with enamel and pebbles.

The American sculptor Alexander Calder, best known for his colourful wire mobiles, was born in Philadelphia and originally studied engineering. By his own account his first jewellery was made for his sister's dolls when he was eight, out of pieces of discarded copper wire. Wire remained an important element in his larger work and his preferred material for jewellery. He worked in both silver and brass, either hammering or twisting the wire to achieve strong, simple forms. Most of his jewellery was made for family and friends rather than for sale. As Carol Hogben wrote in the catalogue for the V&A's exhibition *Modern Artists' Jewels* in 1984, artists 'are not fettered by any of the conventions that strangle all the life out of shop jewels. ... They are free to let their own imaginations leap. Most of their jewels occur as a means of distraction, a relaxation from their real, primary work. It may be, sometimes, a labour of love; or an experiment, more simply, just made for fun.' Calder's jewellery exemplifies this light-hearted genius, and it introduced a highly individual note to jewellery of the 1930s.

Above: Bracelet of chromium-plated brass set with a rectangular panel of haematite. Designed by Naum Slutzky and made in Hamburg, 1929 (length 18cm/7.1in).

Far right: Necklace with flexible pendant, made from linked sections of chromium-plated brass tubing. Designed by Naum Slutzky and made in Hamburg, 1929 (diameter of pendant 8cm/3.1in).

Right: Necklace of conical spirals of brass wire, made by Alexander Calder in Paris, *c.* 1938 (unfastened length 39.4cm/15.5in).

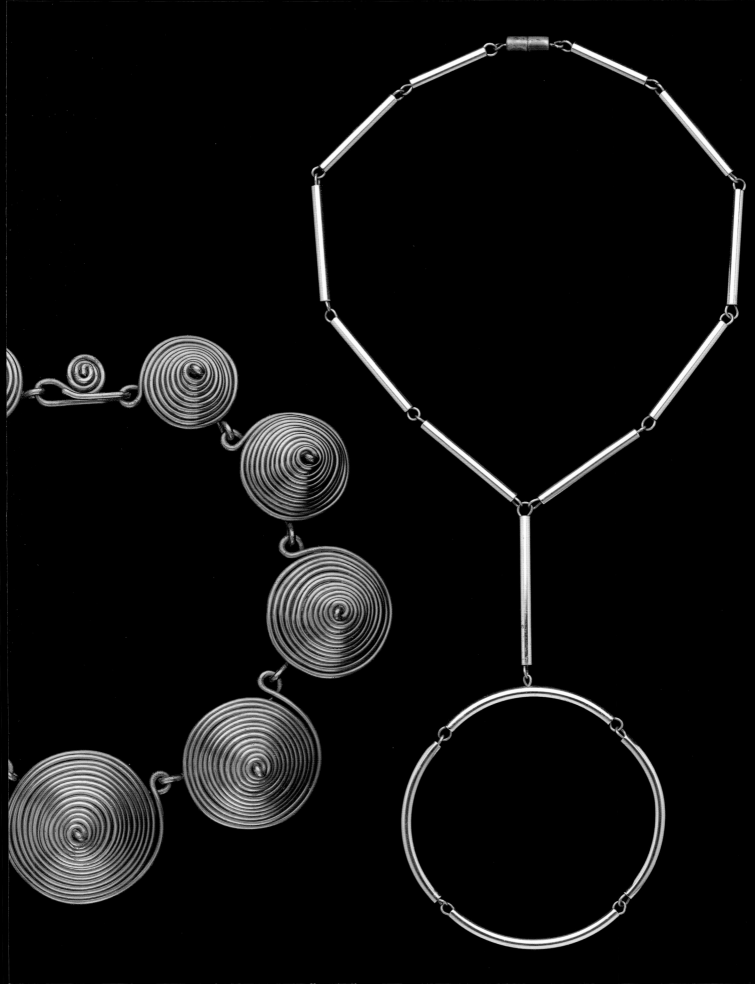

THE POST-WAR DECADE, 1945–55

Jewellery production throughout Europe had been severely affected by the Second World War, and speeds of recovery varied widely across the different countries. In Britain the austerity measures following the War continued to impede the creation of new pieces right through the 1950s. At the time Eyna Podolsky made the necklace illustrated opposite in 1947, the purchase tax on new jewellery – which had peaked at the prohibitive rate of 125 percent – was even applied to basic items such as wedding rings. Nine-carat gold was the Utility Standard for home use, with 18-carat gold possible only in pieces made for export.

Flexible, ribbed tubes of gold had appeared in the late 1930s and remained very fashionable for necklaces and bracelets throughout the 1940s. They were made from interlocking angular links and were known either as 'snakes' or 'gas-pipes', depending on how they were constructed. Gold, which had returned to prominence because of the wartime requisitioning of platinum for the armaments industry, remained fashionable for gem-set jewellery. Bulky abstract motifs were repeated to form bracelets and watch straps, while softer forms of flowers and birds were made in brightly polished gold and colourful gemstones.

Several highly original individuals stand out during this period for their distinctive and innovative contributions to the development of modern jewellery. The German jeweller and teacher Elisabeth Treskow combined technical virtuosity in her execution of granulation, with a superb mastery of form. In 1945 the sculptor Henning Koppel created his first range of silver jewellery for the Danish firm Georg Jensen. The simple, asymmetric organic shapes that he created were of great sculptural beauty and purity, classic examples of what was soon regarded as a distinctive Scandinavian style. Immensely innovative at the time, many have remained in production to this day. In Paris Line Vautrin had established her reputation for chic and artistic jewellery, buttons and boxes made of gilt metal. Her designs were bold and simple, with clever literary references or a subtle wit just beneath the surface.

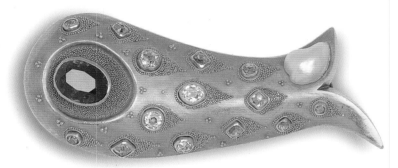

Top: Silver brooch designed by Henning Koppel for Jensen, made in Denmark, c.1950 (height 2.5cm/0.98in).

Above: Brooch in the form of a fish, made of gold decorated with granulation and set with a sapphire, a pearl and diamonds. Designed and made by Elisabeth Treskow in Cologne, 1953 (height 2cm/0.79in).

Below: Belt buckle of gilt bronze by the French designer Line Vautrin, made in Paris, c.1946. Titled *Gendarme et Voleur* it shows a policeman, recognizable by his large moustache and his helmet, in pursuit of a thief. The idea of the chase is emphasized by two dogs leaping over the centre rings and the extended limbs of the figures (length 26.8cm/10.6in).

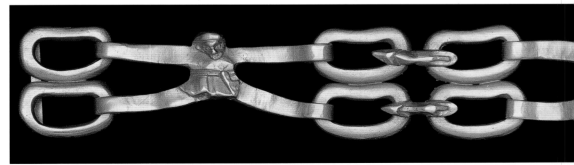

Necklace of white and yellow gold 'snake' chains, set with diamonds, sapphires and rubies. The gem-set scroll and tails in the centre may be detached and worn separately as a clip. Designed and made by Eyna Podolsky for the export market, London, 1947 (unfastened length 39.5cm/ 15.6in).

THE INTERNATIONAL EXHIBITION OF MODERN JEWELLERY, GOLDSMITHS HALL, 1961

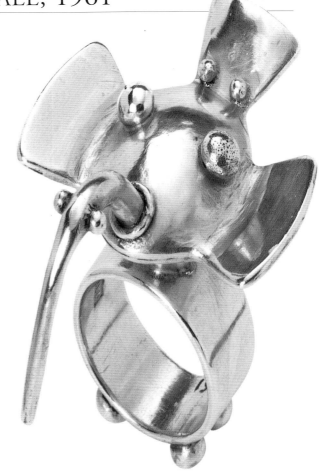

This exhibition, organized jointly by the Worshipful Company of Goldsmiths and the V&A, and curated by Graham Hughes, boasted that it was the world's first international display of modern jewellery. It covered the decades from 1890 to 1961, with over 1000 exhibits representing a tremendous variety of styles, including the first London showing of masterpieces from the Gulbenkian Collection of Lalique's jewellery. The aim of the exhibition was to demonstrate jewellery's artistic potential and to reverse the depressed state of the British jewellery trade, which had suffered greatly both during and after the Second World War due to austerity measures and prohibitive purchase taxes. Because of this promotional aspect there was a very strong emphasis on the contemporary, principally work from Europe and North America but also from countries as distant as Australia, Bolivia and India. Modern diamond jewellery by Gilbert Albert for Patek Philippe, by Harry Winston and by all the major European jewellery houses was shown, alongside work in semi-precious materials by artist–craftsmen and idiosyncratic pieces made as a sideline by painters and sculptors.

Highly original work made over recent decades was contributed by many artists, including Jean Arp, Alexander Calder (see page 114), Giorgio de Chirico, Salvador Dali, Max Ernst, Alberto Giacometti, Pablo Picasso and Yves Tanguy. In addition challenging new work was commissioned from various British artists, who were sent a matchbox full of wax with which to model a jewel, which was then returned to the exhibition organizers for casting in metal. These artists' pieces, often rough-textured and heavy, added a fascinating and new dimension and, as the exhibition catalogue stated, 'proved, if proof be needed, that cheap materials need not mean artistic insignificance, and that creative imagination shown with one visual art can very often be diverted to another'. These were important lessons, recognizing alternative priorities within jewellery, and helped to consolidate the position of the emerging artist–jewellery movement. Across Europe jewellers such as Friedrich Becker, Torun Bülow Hübe, John Donald, Gerda Flöckinger and E. R. Nele had recently established small studios in which they designed and made their own distinctive work. All of these craftsmen exhibited in 1961, providing a vital stimulus to art and design students and exerting a considerable influence on developments within jewellery over the succeeding years.

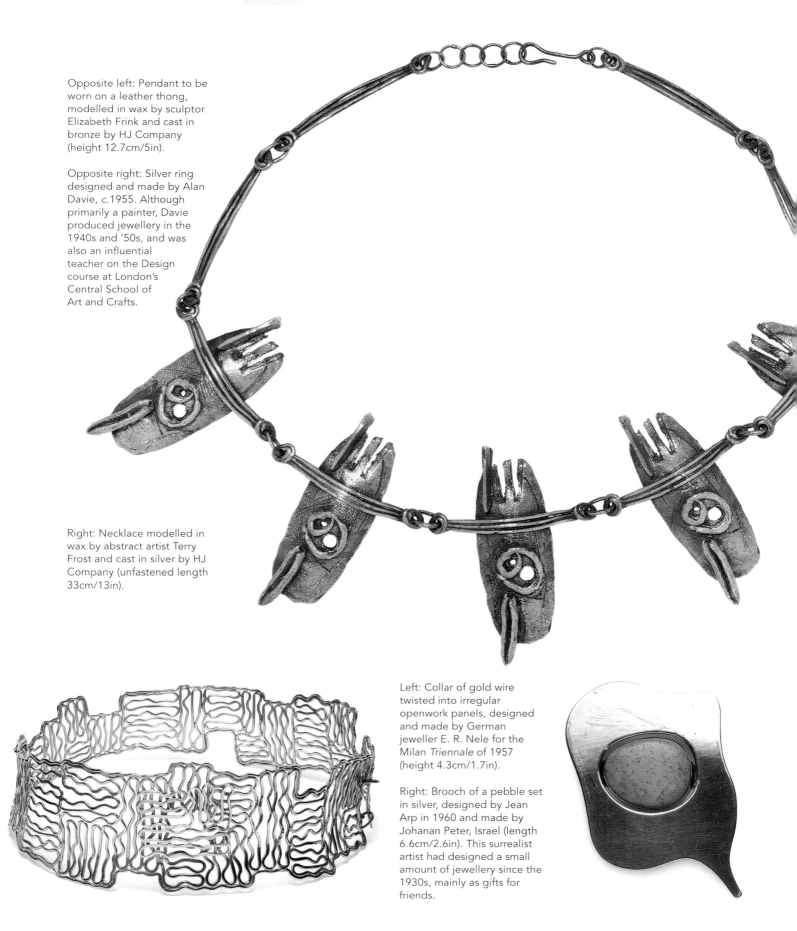

Opposite left: Pendant to be worn on a leather thong, modelled in wax by sculptor Elizabeth Frink and cast in bronze by HJ Company (height 12.7cm/5in).

Opposite right: Silver ring designed and made by Alan Davie, c.1955. Although primarily a painter, Davie produced jewellery in the 1940s and '50s, and was also an influential teacher on the Design course at London's Central School of Art and Crafts.

Right: Necklace modelled in wax by abstract artist Terry Frost and cast in silver by HJ Company (unfastened length 33cm/13in).

Left: Collar of gold wire twisted into irregular openwork panels, designed and made by German jeweller E. R. Nele for the Milan *Triennale* of 1957 (height 4.3cm/1.7in).

Right: Brooch of a pebble set in silver, designed by Jean Arp in 1960 and made by Johanan Peter, Israel (length 6.6cm/2.6in). This surrealist artist had designed a small amount of jewellery since the 1930s, mainly as gifts for friends.

THE 1960s

The more valuable the stone, the more unimaginative the setting: this is the unwritten rule for both buyer and manufacturer, based on a solid convention of what will sell. However the convention is now being challenged in this country by a few enterprising jewellers who are sensitive about the designs they produce; by a handful of retailers who dare to stock their goods; by the patrons who help to keep them in business, and by the designers whose work ... has helped to create the demand for beautiful jewellery.

GILLIAN NAYLOR, 'DIAMONDS ARE FOR DOWAGERS', *DESIGN MAGAZINE*, FEBRUARY 1962

Below: Brooch *Les Fils d'Éos*, designed by the artist Georges Braque and made by the jeweller Heger de Loewenfeld in France in 1963 (height 3.5cm/1.4in). The three birds, of polished lapis lazuli, textured gold and diamonds pavé-set in platinum, represent the three sons of Eos, goddess of the dawn: Phaethon, the guardian of Aphrodite's temple; Phosphorus, the morning star, and Hesperus, the evening star. The collaboration between Braque and de Loewenfeld dates from the final years of Braque's life when he was in his eighties. De Loewenfeld would prepare designs from Braque's existing work, and Braque would sign the ones he approved. The source for this particular brooch has been identified as the lithograph used on the cover of *Cinq poésies en hommage à Georges Braque* by René Char (Geneva, 1958). Braque, who mixed sand into his paint to create a granular effect, disliked shiny gold, and so de Loewenfeld developed a gritty matt finish to the metal by fusing gold on gold. This type of textured surface was to become a highly fashionable and distinctive feature of jewellery made in the 1960s.

Above: Brooch of silver, 'oxidized' in parts, designed and made by John Donald, England, in 1960–61 (height 4.8cm/1.9in). John Donald studied graphic art at Farnham School of Art followed by jewellery at the Royal College of Art, then set up his London workshop in 1961. He is best known for his innovative work in gold, with which he achieved a great variety of textures and forms, in some cases by dropping molten gold into water, or, alternatively, mirroring striations and structures within nature. His work typically incorporates a rich variety of gemstones, which – particularly in pieces of the late 1960s and 1970s – are often unfaceted or left in their natural crystal form.

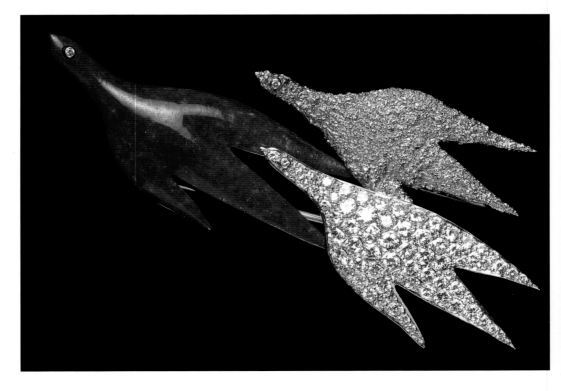

Necklet of 14 carat gold and pearls, designed and made by Gerda Flöckinger, England, 1960 (total height 24.7cm/9.7in). This was the first piece of contemporary jewellery commissioned by the Museum, a choice that recognized Gerda Flöckinger's pre-eminence in the emerging alternative jewellery scene in London. Born in Innsbruck in 1927, she emigrated to England in 1938. She studied fine art at St Martin's School of Art, and jewellery and enamels at Central School of Arts and Crafts. On leaving in 1956 she took the then highly unusual decision to work as an independent designer and maker. In 1962 she established the pioneering course in experimental jewellery at Hornsey School of Art, where many of the next generation of British artist–jewellers were taught.

Top left: Ring of 'oxidized' silver and gold, set with a carved citrine, a tourmaline and an opal, designed and made by Gerda Flöckinger in 1969. The flat polished surfaces of Flöckinger's early pieces have made way for the encrusted, organic textures that have come to typify her work. At this date large unusual stones – cameos, soft-coloured cabochons, veined turquoises and irregular pearls – were incorporated to give glowing pools of colour amidst the swirling metal.

Centre: Gold and diamond ring, designed by Jeanne Thé, London, 1964. Born in Java in 1941 Jeanne Thé trained in metalwork and jewellery in Stuttgart and London. On graduating she worked for several years with Andrew Grima, before establishing her own workshop in 1964, the same year this ring won third prize in the De Beers engagement-ring competition.

Bottom: Brooch of gold set with diamonds, designed by Louis Osman in 1965 as the focal point of a large hand-beaten silver centrepiece where, when not being worn, it rests beneath a square of polished rock crystal (height 4.3cm/1.7in). In a letter to the original owner Osman wrote that 'the jewel is of "fine" (i.e. absolutely pure) gold: the design exploits its softness & beautiful colour.' This softness is expressed principally in the crumpled texture of the metal, a very fashionable surface treatment in the mid-1960s. Louis Osman, born in 1914, was one of the major English silversmiths of the immediate post-war generation. He trained as an architect at the Bartlett School of Architecture and then studied at the Slade School of Art. In 1969 he designed and made the coronet worn by Prince Charles at his investiture as Prince of Wales.

Opposite
Top: Bracelet made from a clear acrylic disc slit in the middle with the edges pushed out through which to allow the wrist to pass, designed and made by Gijs Bakker, Holland, 1967 (diameter 11.5cm/4.5in). Bakker was born in 1942 and studied at the Amsterdam Academy of Art and the Kunstfack Skolen in Stockholm. He was one of the first of the artist–jewellers to experiment with synthetic and non-precious materials in the late 1960s and early '70s, and, with his wife Emmy van Leersum, dominated the radical jewellery scene in Holland.

Bottom: Necklace of black Cornish pebbles set in silver, designed and made by Helga Zahn in England, 1966–7 (height 16.5cm/ 6.5in). Helga Zahn was born in Germany in 1936 and came to England in 1957, studying at Leeds College of Arts, then at Central School of Arts and Crafts. She concentrated originally on painting and printmaking but became an influential figure in the British contemporary-jewellery scene in the 1960s, her distinctive style diverging strikingly from conventional notions of jewellery. Her work uses strong, simple forms, informally arranged and executed on a bold scale, and often incorporates found objects such as stones and arrowheads.

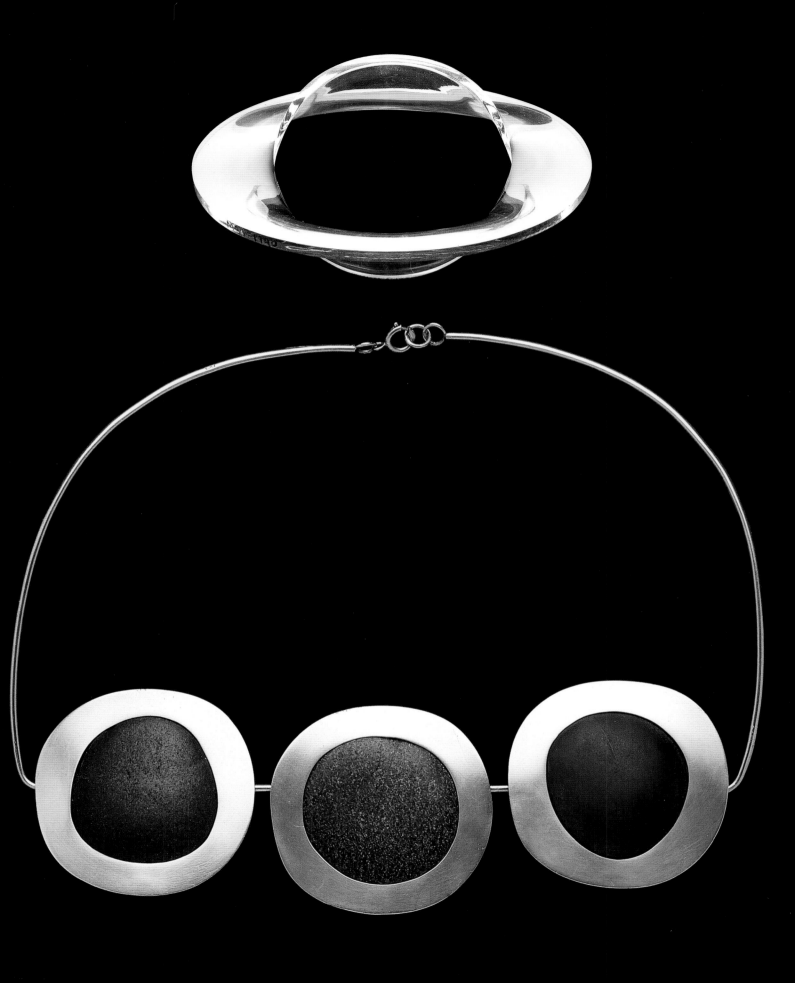

THE 1970S

By the early 1970s, the last vestiges of etiquette in clothing and jewellery had really disappeared: 'anything goes'. Although there were still social groups, it was hard to distinguish them by their jewellery. For some people, it will always be important to have very expensive, precious jewellery, but this is now a matter of personal choice (and of being able to afford it) rather than a social 'must'.

BARBARA CARTLIDGE, *TWENTIETH-CENTURY JEWELRY* (1985)

Below: Bracelet of steel and acrylic, designed and made by Gerd Rothmann, Germany, 1970 (height of central panel 6cm/2.4in). The bracelet was intended to be part of a multiple set: the decorative panel, here a bagatelle game, slides off and may be substituted with another panel. This is not a unique piece but part of a limited edition of 50. Rothmann, who was born in 1941, studied at the Staatlichen Zeichenakademie in Hanau. He was one of a small group of pioneering artist–craftsmen who in the early 1970s promoted the use of acrylic in jewellery, a material that complemented his enthusiasm for Pop art.

Right: Necklace of enamelled gold, designed and made by Wendy Ramshaw, England, 1971, part of the collection with which she won the Council of Industrial Design Award in 1972 (height 18.5cm/7.3in). She is the only jeweller to have won this award, whose criteria were 'technical innovation, fitness for purpose, ease of use and good appearance'. The *Connoisseur* in June 1972 commented on the almost mechanically precise lines of her work: 'There isn't a beaten or textured surface anywhere and no facets to flash and sparkle and break the smooth continuous curves.' Born in 1939, Wendy Ramshaw studied illustration and fabric design at Newcastle College of Art and Design, followed by a year at Reading University and postgraduate studies at the Central School of Art and Design, London. Her first jewellery was made in 1960, and during the following decade she and her husband David Watkins collaborated on jewellery made of screenprinted perspex and self-assembly packs of paper jewellery. Only around 1970 did she start to work seriously in silver and gold, and to establish her distinctive modernist style. She is best known for the multiple-ring sets made up of co-ordinating rings, which, when not being worn, are displayed as small sculptures on lathe-turned stands.

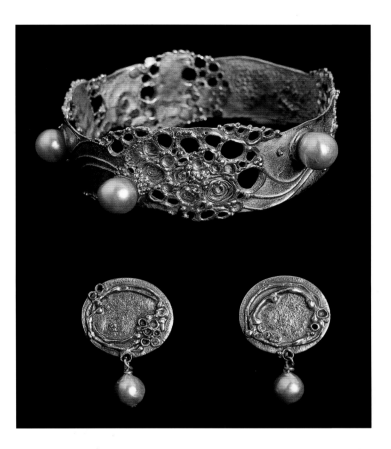

Right: Bracelet and earrings of undulating silver, swirling and bubbling like an arrested stream of molten metal, set with grey cultured pearls irregularly spaced in crater-like settings. Designed and made by Gerda Flöckinger, England, 1973 and 1975 (diameter 8.5cm/ 3.3in). The influences of landscape, Klimt's paintings and the Viennese Secession may be glimpsed in her work, which delights and surprises with its spontaneity of form. The pitted surfaces are created by controlled melting of the metal, while the curving lines of wire are fused rather than soldered for subtler effect. Gerda Flöckinger was the first contemporary jeweller to be given her own exhibition at the V&A in 1971, and her continuing contribution to British jewellery was recognized in 1991 when she was awarded a CBE.

Below right: Ring of silver and acrylic, designed and made by Fritz Maierhofer, Austria, 1973. The design reflects Maierhofer's concern with geometry, while the central ball-and-socket joint and the three discs, grooved to look like screw heads, show his interest in construction. Maierhofer was born in 1941 in Vienna, where he served a conventional jeweller's apprenticeship with the firm of Anton Heldwein. After three years working for Andrew Grima in London he went freelance in 1970 and immediately began to experiment, combining acrylic with precious metals. His work in acrylic was first seen in London at an exhibition with Gerd Rothmann and Claus Bury at the Electrum Gallery in 1971 – it was immensely influential and demonstrated the creative potential of acrylics.

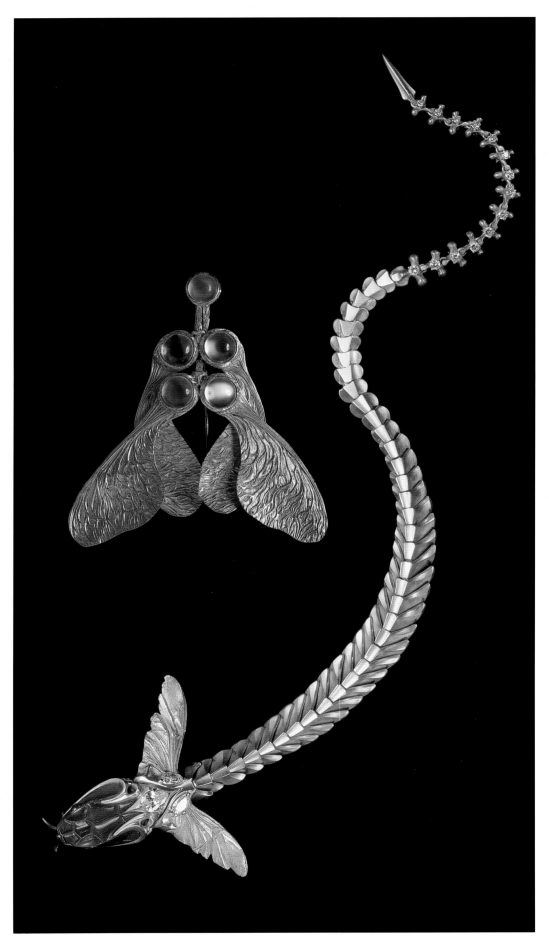

Far left: Brooch of gold sycamore seeds set with moonstones, designed by Malcolm Appleby and made by Roger Doyle, England, 1975 (height 5.8cm/2.3in). Malcolm Appleby, born in 1946, studied at Ravensbourne College, Sir John Cass School of Art and the Royal College of Art. Since 1969 he has been based in Scotland. Equally renowned for his silver designs and the fantastical imagery of his virtuoso engraving, his jewellery, whether of steel or engraved gold and silver, expresses the wild beauty of the natural world.

Left: Bracelet of a winged serpent, designed and made by Courts & Hackett, England, 1975 (length 27.3cm/10.7in). The articulated gold body of the serpent wraps around the wearer's wrist, and the diamond-set tail is gripped in its jaws by a clasp within the carved buffalo-horn head. It has ruby eyes and three large diamonds set at its neck. David Courts, born in 1945, and Bill Hackett, born in 1949, trained at Hornsey College of Art and the Royal College of Art. They have been in partnership since 1974, producing exquisitely crafted pieces often with a slightly macabre twist.

Right: Neckpiece of acrylic decorated with gold discs, designed and made by David Watkins, England, 1975 (height 27cm/10.6in). Watkins was born in 1940 and studied Fine Art at Reading University. He works as a sculptor as well as a jeweller and is the professor of silversmithing and jewellery at the Royal College of Art. His precise, minimal style is inspired by technological imagery, and neckpieces remain his most characteristic pieces.

Above: Brooch of titanium in a silver frame, designed and made by Edward de Large, England, 1977 (height 5.6cm/2.2in). De Large was born in 1949 and studied at Camberwell School of Art and the Royal College of Art. The intense colours of his 'cloudscapes' were created by passing a controlled electric current over the surface of a titanium sheet. On this very flat piece the illusion of a third dimension is created by the shadowy box that can only be seen from certain angles. The colouring of refractory metals had become popular by the mid-1980s, but such sophisticated effects are rare.

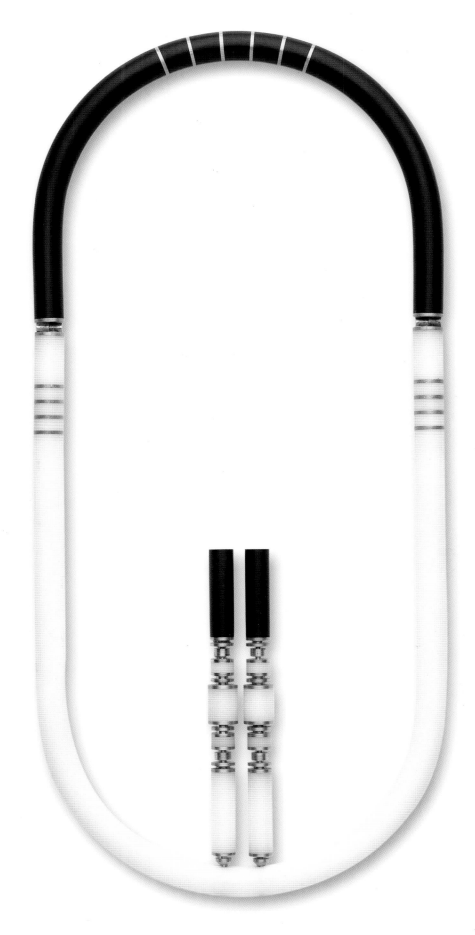

THE 1980S

If materials are of greater significance than the thought which they are used to convey then we have missed our road.

DAVID POSTON, *CRAFTS* MAGAZINE, SEPTEMBER/OCTOBER 1983

Above: Necklace of blue-black steel 'feathers' and gold pod-shaped pendants held by an underlying silver mesh, designed and made by Tone Vigeland, Norway, 1983 (depth of fringe 8.5cm/3.3in). Vigeland described how 'a friend from Bergen came to see me with a set of black iron nails. I found that when I hammered them flat, they had a lovely character – almost like black feathers. So in this case first I discovered the material, and then I found a design to suit it.' Vigeland was born in 1938 and studied at the Kunst und Handverksskolen and the Yrkesskole, both in Oslo. Her later work is typically made up of many similar, small elements, which are ingeniously linked together to create unexpectedly flexible and clinging sculptural forms.

Above: Cravat brooch of knitted silver wire, designed and made by Arline Fisch, America, 1980 (length 28 cm/11in). Fisch, born in 1931, trained at Skidmore College, New York, and the University of Illinois, and was for many years professor at San Diego State University. Since the mid-1970s she has been best known for applying textile techniques such as knitting and weaving to precious metals. This large bodice ornament, designed to be pinned to the neckline or to a ribbon around the neck, was inspired by the V&A's intricate lace cravat carved out of limewood by Grinling Gibbons at the end of the seventeenth century.

Right: Pendant or brooch of silver, gold and perspex, made by Vicky Ambery-Smith, England, 1980 (height 6.3cm/2.5in). Vicky Ambery-Smith was born in 1955 and trained at Hornsey College of Art. She specializes in architectural themes – creating accurate models of known buildings or less precise pieces, representing architectural details. This particular jewel is based on Brunelleschi's unrealized design for St Peter's, Rome. One side is cut away to show the internal structure of the building, while the floor-plan of the apse descends in an arc below.

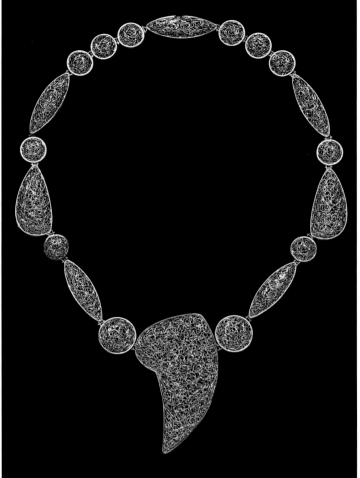

Left: Necklace of papier-mâché beads made from Chinese newspaper and gold foil, designed and made by Robert Ebendorf, America, 1985 (diameter of individual beads 5cm/2in). Ebendorf was born in 1938 and studied at the University of Kansas. An early enthusiast for incorporating 'found' materials in jewellery, he has taught widely in America – notably at the State University of New York, New Paltz, where he was Professor of Art for many years.

Above: Necklace of platinum filigree with glints of 24-carat gold, designed and made by Jacqueline Mina, London, 1986 (height 17.5cm/6.9in). Mina has been at the forefront of new work in platinum, a difficult metal, with which she has achieved effects of great subtlety and beauty. She described this piece as 'light and lacy, yet with clear outlines of smooth, shiny platinum wire, closer inspection reveals the construction to be of tiny "rosettes" connected with hundreds of tiny splashes of fine gold glinting amongst the white sparkling platinum'. She was born in 1942 and studied at Hornsey College of Art and the Royal College of Art.

THE 1980S

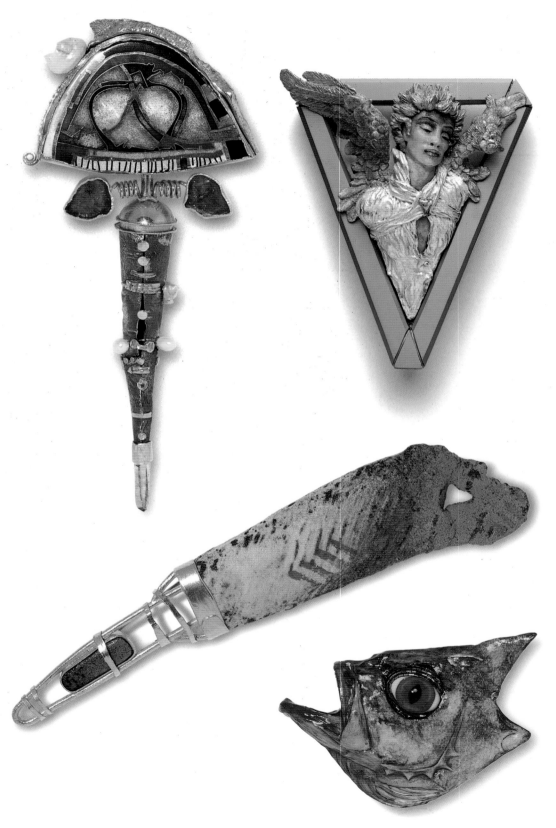

Top left: Brooch *Virgin and the Unicorn* of gold, silver, enamel, pearls, amethyst and lead. Designed and made by William Harper, America, 1988 (height 16.5cm/6.5in). Harper was born in 1944 and attended Western Reserve University and Cleveland Institute of Art. He is one of the finest contemporary enamellers, and this piece is typical of his work with its wide range of materials and textures, and the mystical ideas that underlie its composition.

Top right: Brooch *Seraph*, designed and made by Kevin Coates, England, 1989 (height 6.6cm/2.6in). Within the titanium frame, the face of the figure is of carved opal, his garments of silver, his wings of patinated silver and his hair of gold. Coates has explained that the figure 'is from the red-winged order of Seraphim – highest in the ninefold hierarchies of Angels. Associated with light and purity, the Seraph is sent to inspire mankind with the gift of Divine Love.' Coates was born in 1950 and studied music before training in jewellery at the Central School of Art and Design. His work is distinguished by the intellectual complexity of the references underlying each piece. It is predominantly figurative and demonstrates his virtuosity across an extraordinary variety of materials.

Centre: Brooch *Priori 25* of enamel, copper and gold, made by Jamie Bennett, America, 1989 (height 12.9cm/5.1in). Bennett was born in 1948 and trained at the University of Georgia and the State University of New York, New Paltz, where he is now a professor. His enamelwork is distinctively matt and granular, and the

Priori series explored the use of enamelling in three dimensions on a hollow, electroformed copper core.

Opposite bottom: Fish-head brooch made from the preserved head of a red bream, designed and made by Simon Costin, England, 1988 (height 7.9cm/3.1in). The preserved fish-head has been lined with gold leaf and set with a glass eye surrounded by Venetian glass beads. Costin was born in 1962 and began to study taxidermy as a schoolchild at classes held by the Natural History Museum. He is also trained in theatre design. At the time the V&A commissioned this brooch his studio was in a squat, and his first version was destroyed by rats.

Below: Steel bracelet set with a bar of synthetic sapphire, designed and made by Friedrich Becker, Germany, 1988 (height 7.7cm/3in). Becker trained as an aeronautical engineer before studying jewellery at the Werkkunstschule in Düsseldorf. In 1959 he explained that 'professionally speaking, my home is neither in the sphere of free artistic endeavour nor in the field of artistic craftsmanship, but rather in the world of machinery construction and aerospace technology.' The fine precision required in this industry is reflected in his exact, turned forms and is even more evident in his kinetic jewellery – with its moving parts circling around concentric and non-concentric bearings.

THE 1980S

Below: Necklace of carved jade, coral and seed pearls, designed and made by Charlotte de Syllas, England, 1989 (height of shell clasp 4.5cm/1.8in). De Syllas, born in 1946, trained at Hornsey College of Art under Gerda Flöckinger and specializes in the carving of hardstones.

The central pair of nephrite cockle shells are lined with silver and open to act as the clasp. The snail shells above, of coral and nephrite, are inlaid with silver lines, as is the white jadeite shell at the top that holds secure the silk threads on which the pearls are threaded. This silk – orange to match the coral on the left and green to match the jadeite on the right – gives a subtle colouring to the translucent seed-pearls. It was dyed and braided by Catherine Martin according to classical Japanese techniques.

Opposite: Neckpiece of 'oxidized' silver and black acrylic, designed and made by Wendy Ramshaw, England, 1989, as part of her Picasso's Ladies series (diameter 35cm/13.8in). The neckpiece was designed after a pencil drawing of Françoise Gilot that Picasso made in July 1946, the 'oxidized' silver echoing the dark pencil lines. Ramshaw explains that the shapes 'embrace a number of dissimilar elements inspired directly by the Picasso drawing. One of the elements is like a large rigid feather, another a black cloud suspended amongst zigzags, and a spiral with a terminal. ... If placed on the drawn image, [it] would combine with the marks of the pencil and surround the head like a ring of complex drawn lines'. Ramshaw, one of the most influential of British jewellers, was awarded an OBE in 1993. Her recent work includes designs for architectural ironwork, notably the gate for St John's College, Oxford, and the screen for the V&A's staff restaurant.

THE 1990S

S tudio jewellery is characterized by a concern for individuality. ...The work may be made in a wide range of materials, in many forms, and may communicate a vast array of different ideas, but the valuing of the individual is an underlying concern.
AMANDA GAME AND ELIZABETH GORING, *JEWELLERY MOVES*, CATALOGUE FOR THE NATIONAL MUSEUMS OF SCOTLAND, 1998

Below left: Brooch of gold, designed and made by Yasuki Hiramatsu, Japan, in 1990 (height 3.3cm/1.3in). The thin gold foil has been crumpled, softening the angularity of the square and illustrating the Japanese fascination with surface textures. Hiramatsu was born in 1926 into a family of traditional metalworkers. He studied at Tokyo National University of Fine Arts and Music, where he went on to become a professor. Although the Japanese have a rich history of metalworking they have no jewellery tradition, and in the period after the Second World War Hiramatsu was a pivotal figure in establishing contemporary jewellery in Japan.

Below right: Brooch *Impressions* with companion ring, silver, the band of the ring in stainless steel, designed and made by Elisabeth Holder, Germany, 1991 and 1990 (height of the brooch 7.6cm/3in). The restrained angular decoration on the brooch is directly derived from the ring, which was impressed into modelling clay at different angles to make the mould for the oval panel of the brooch. This hidden presence of one jewel within another was a concept that intrigued Holder, and one that she explored in the Impressions series. Elisabeth Holder trained at the Fachhochschule, Düsseldorf, where she is now a professor, and at the Royal College of Art.

Right: Necklace of gilded silver, silver, lapis lazuli, chalcedony, haematite and granite, designed and made by Hermann Jünger, Germany, 1990 (length of central gilded bar 8.1cm/3.2in). One of Jünger's distinctive necklace sets, where a selection of metals and stones are polished into smooth, geometric forms and drilled so that they may be threaded on to a flexible gold wire. The wearer chooses the order in which they are threaded, and when not being worn the pieces are arranged in the compartments of their box where they may be enjoyed as a sculpture. Jünger was born in 1928 and trained at the Zeichenakademie in Hanau and the Akademie der Bildenden Künste, Munich.

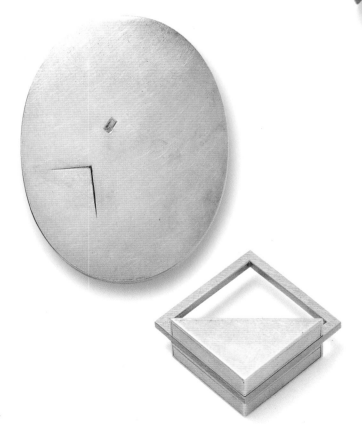

Bracelet of gold, designed and made by Giampaolo Babetto, Italy, 1990 (height 5.3cm/2.1in). The rich colour is due to the blend of silver and copper that Babetto has mixed with the pure gold, while the subtle texture comes from repeated heating and dipping in acid, followed by beating the surfaces with the flat end of a hammer. Babetto was born in 1947 and studied at the Instituto d'Arte Pietro Selvatico in Padua and the Accademia di Belle Arti in Venice. His studio is in Padua, the principal centre for contemporary studio jewellery in Italy.

THE 1990s

Necklace of coral, gold and cornelian, designed and made by Breon O'Casey, England, 1990–91 (length of gold rays c.11 cm/4.3in). O'Casey, born in 1928, trained originally as a sculptor but also paints, weaves and works with metals. He has been making jewellery since 1960, two years after he moved to St Ives, where he worked first as an assistant to Dennis Mitchell and Dame Barbara Hepworth. He has long been established as a distinctive and influential presence in contemporary jewellery, known in particular for the hand-beaten, almost primitive appearance of his metalwork and for his incorporating richly coloured materials, such as lapis lazuli, coral and sandblasted-gemstone beads.

Below: Earrings of platinum wire, braided according to the Japanese silk-braiding technique of *kumihimo*, designed and made by Catherine Martin, England, 1991 (height 10 cm/4in). Martin, born in 1949, trained initially as a musician. While in Japan she learnt classical

Japanese braiding at the Domyo School of Kumihimo and some years later went to the Sir John Cass School of Art and then the Royal College of Art to study jewellery. These are the first pieces she made by this technique. She currently uses mainly gold wire, principally making earrings and necklaces

Right: Brooch made of acrylic and polyester, designed and made by Peter Chang, Scotland, 1992 (height 17.2cm/6.8in). Although this appears as a smooth and

seamless whole, the brooch is put together from many separate elements: the red spots and pink discs in the middle section are turned on a lathe from acrylic sheet that is more commonly used for shop signs, the spaces between are of resin. Almost

all the materials used are recycled but with an artistry that disguises their origins and transforms their identities. Chang, born in 1944, trained as a sculptor at Liverpool School of Art and the Slade School. He has been making jewellery since the early 1970s.

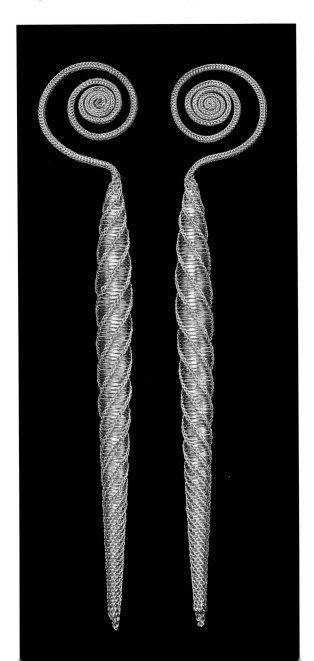

THE 1990S

Above: Bracelet *Mediterranean* of silver, diamonds and reused 'bus stop' signs, designed and made by ROY, America, 1994 (length 16.9cm/9.7in). A silversmith as well as a jeweller, ROY was born in 1962 and trained at the Carnegie Mellon University, Pittsburg, and Kent State University, Ohio. While not rejecting more precious materials, recycling is a major aspect of her work, and her use of colourful aluminium street signs mounted in hinged bracelet panels is particularly successful.

Below: Neckpiece *Ring of Fire* of painted papier-mâché, designed and made by Marjorie Schick, America, 1995 (diameter 50.5cm/20in). Schick was born in 1941 and studied at the University of Wisconsin, Indiana University and the Sir John Cass School of Art, London. She is currently a professor at Pittsburg State University. She describes her work as 'a sculptural statement, which is complete when off the figure yet is constructed and exists because of the human body'.

Opposite: Three necklaces from the Winter series, of 'oxidized' silver, designed and made by Cynthia Cousens, England, 1996 (length of twig pendant on central necklace 24cm/9.4in). Cousens was born in 1956 and trained at Loughborough College of Art and the Royal College of Art. These pieces, starkly reflecting the desolation of the winter landscape, originated in drawings done on the South Downs. The top necklace, made from a flattened tube of knitted silver wire and designed to be worn like a scarf, is titled *Briar*. In the middle, of adjustable length, is *Twig*, with its delicate openwork pendant attached to the punched cylindrical beads with a twist of silver resembling raffia. Below is *Garland Nest*, a delicate yet unruly wreath of lines and ends made up of linked chevron forms, which closely resemble the paired needles of the Scots Pine

PART III

MANUFACTURING AND DISTRIBUTION

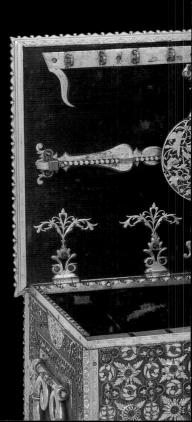

HALLMARKING AND DESIGN REGISTRATION

'Scottish pebble' brooch made of silver (diameter 5.1cm/2in). The Registry mark on the back reveals that the design was registered on 14 October 1865 by James Fenton, a Birmingham manufacturer.

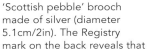

The assaying and hallmarking of precious metals was introduced at an early date in some parts of Europe as a form of quality control and guarantee that the pieces met approved standards of purity. The 1327 charter of the Goldsmiths' Company of London warned of those goldsmiths 'who keep their shops in dark lanes and obscure streets [and] make counterfeit articles of gold and silver … and put more alloy in the silver than they should do' and aimed to prevent such fraud. At different periods and in different countries a range of standards have been adopted for silver and gold (and much later for platinum), and each has had a different mark to distinguish the more valuable or purer alloys from the cheaper ones.

However, for much of history jewellery has been exempted from hallmarking because of its small size and the difficulties of stamping the necessary punches into such delicate work. In England in 1738 the Plate Offences Act expressly exempted from hallmarking all 'Jeweller's Works' except for mourning rings, although other pieces, often rings, were sometimes sent for assaying. In 1855 the requirement for hallmarking was extended to wedding rings, but little other jewellery passed through the English

assay offices during the nineteenth century. American gold jewellery of the nineteenth century was sometimes stamped with a quality mark, but these were not recognized or regulated until 1906. As Americans measure gold in karats, the pieces are stamped with a 'k' (for example 14k). In contrast nineteenth-century French work is invariably marked with a quality mark and a distinctive lozenge-shaped maker's mark, following legislation introduced in the aftermath of the Revolution.

During the nineteenth century manufacturers in all areas became concerned about the copying of their designs by competitors. In England the Designs Acts were introduced in 1842, giving three years' protection to all new jewellery designs lodged with the Registrar of Designs (these records are now at the Public Record Office). Pieces that enjoyed this protection carried a diamond mark, with the details encoded in letters, or a registered number. Another stamp indicating patent protection was *DÉPOSÉ*, which was often used by German jewellers. In addition to protecting designs, many European and American patents were taken out on technical innovations in manufacturing processes and for improved clasps and fastenings.

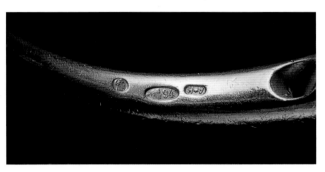

Above: Mourning ring of gold and enamel commemorating the death of James Selby Pennington in 1831. The central mark denotes the maker or sponsor – the York firm of Barber, Cattle and North. On the left is the King's head or duty mark, and on the right is the date letter for 1831.

Above: Details of the hallmarks on a Fabergé bracelet (see page 83). Above is the name of Fabergé in Cyrillic; the central punch below is known as the *kokoshnik* mark after the woman's headdress – the '*α*' indicates St Petersburg, the woman faces right for 1908–17, and the '94' is the gold quality in *zolotniks* – equivalent to approximately 23 carats; alongside are the initials of the workmaster August Hollming.

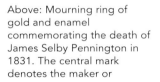

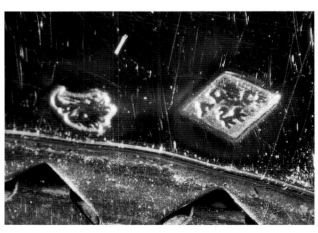

Above: Gold bracelet, c.1870–80 (height of buckle 2.9cm/1.1in). Right: Its hallmarks – this form of the eagle's head is the French restricted warranty mark for gold in use since 1847; the lozenge-shaped maker's mark contains the initials AL and a lion, for the Parisian jeweller Auguste Lion.

SHOPS

From a German Book of Trades, this illustration shows the inside of a sixteenth-century goldsmith's shop.

In medieval times the goldsmith's shop and workshop were often one and the same – engravings and paintings typically show the craftsman working in the window alongside a display of finished goods that were for sale. Even at this date not everything displayed would have necessarily been made on the premises: smaller items such as rings were often bought in from itinerant jewellers or from fairs. However, the frequent presence of raw materials and unmounted gemstones indicate that many pieces were made to commission in the shop. Alternative places for purchasing jewellery included the principal European fairs, such as those at Lagny in Champagne or that held in Paris on All Saints Day. Mercers also sold jewellery – such as girdles and chaplets, where a textile base was adorned with pearls, precious stones and gold thread.

By the late seventeenth century more of a distinction between workshop and showroom had emerged, and during the eighteenth century shops became increasingly opulent. Daniel Defoe in *The Complete English Tradesman* (1726) commented disapprovingly of tradesmen spending two-thirds of their capital 'in painting and gilding, in fine shelves, shutters, pediments, columns of the several orders of architecture, and the like'. He regarded as absurd the spending of 'two or three, nay, five hundred pounds, to fit up what we may call the outside of a shop', but it was clearly an investment that the retailers, who realized how the right atmosphere could encourage greater extravagance in their customers, considered worthwhile. Such was their success that calling at fashionable shops became a favourite society pastime, and in the late eighteenth century the road on Ludgate Hill was often blocked by carriages waiting outside Rundell's celebrated shop. The delights within, where 'Gold and silver dishes were neatly arranged on shelves which reached the ceiling: expensive ropes of diamonds, rubies, emeralds, corals and pearls outshone the stars' were recorded by the Persian ambassador who visited in 1810. Similar opulence characterized the luxury trades in the rest of Europe, although the manufacturer Matthew Boulton commented that in Paris 'all their finest shops are upstairs', an arrangement that perhaps gave greater privacy than the glazed windows at street level more usual in London shops.

The *Illustrated London News* of 17 November 1860 gives a full description of Harry Emanuel's imposing new shop in Hanover Square, indicating what was expected then of a top London jeweller. It mentions the basement's 'strong iron and fireproof keeps, in which are deposited every night the most costly jewels and precious stones'. Upstairs the large showroom was decorated with an ornamental stove, extravagant flower arrangements, glass and ebony cabinets, and a painted plaster cornice decorated with emeralds, rubies and amethysts. Of greater fame and individuality was Castellani's shop in Rome, which became something of a tourist attraction in

its own right. The family's scholarly interest in archaeology enabled them to display their modern jewellery alongside antique vases and other works of art.

Dramatic interiors were also created by the Art Nouveau jewellers of Paris. Fouquet's exotic shop of 1901 was designed by the Czech artist Alphonse Mucha, who also designed some of their jewellery. The outside was dominated by a large bronze panel of a bejewelled female figure, and within swirling, colourful decoration covered every surface. Similarly, Lalique extended the spirit that pervades his jewellery into his showcases, exhibition stands and shop. His new house, workshop and showroom of 1902 explored the forms of pine trees through its masonry, glass and ironwork, while the chandeliers were serpents and chameleons, the light shining through their eyes.

Top left: The façade of Hawley's jewellery shop on the Strand, c.1800. Larger items occupy the upper shelves while the jewellery, including necklaces, earrings, wedding hoops and fancy rings, is displayed below. They also advertise repairs, seal engraving and 'likenesses taken in a superior style for 2 guineas'.

Left: The interior of Fouquet's shop on the rue Royale, Paris, designed by Alphonse Mucha, c.1900. Themes and forms from his posters were echoed in the rich decorative scheme, which has been preserved in the Musée Carnavalet, Paris.

TRACING A JEWEL'S HISTORY

Collection of ruby and diamond jewellery, many of the cabochon rubies originating from Tipu Sultan's treasury at Seringapatam. In several different styles, the necklace, brooch and bracelet were made during the late nineteenth century, the earrings and ring at different points between 1920 and 1950.

Throughout history jewellery has been continually recycled – the stones prized out of their mounts, perhaps re-cut and then re-set in the latest style, while the precious metal settings have gone back into the goldsmith's melting pot, their value being set against the cost of the new piece. Occasionally such operations are documented: in the jewellery inventory of James I's consort, Anne of Denmark, there are many such annotations. Of item 239, a set of 34 enamelled gold aglets or Renaissance dress ornaments, we are told that they were 'Deliuered to Sir John Spillman the 27th of Aprile 1610. By her Majesties Comaundement, to be imployed for the making of a Gold Salt'. Similarly in the eighteenth and nineteenth centuries, both family papers

and contemporary novels indicate that the re-setting of inherited gems was a standard procedure. When in Anthony Trollope's novel *The Eustace Diamonds* (1873) Sir Florian gives his new bride the family necklace to wear, he comments 'That setting was done for my mother but it is already old. When we are at home again they shall be reset.' As a result of this practice it is only a very small proportion of jewellery from any period that has survived to the present day, although many pieces contain some elements, and certainly the raw materials, from a succession of earlier jewels.

Regular re-setting combined with the rarity of finding hallmarks on jewellery can make it very difficult to trace the origin of a particular jewel, especially at times when styles were international and slow to change. Where a piece has remained within one family, marriage dates, portraits and family papers can help to unravel its history. An interesting case study is that of the Seringapatam jewels worn by successive generations of the Harris family of Belmont, Kent. Major-General George Harris, Commander-in-Chief of the Madras Presidency, had been awarded £130,000 in prize money following his victory over the great Tipu Sultan of Mysore in southern India in 1799. Much of this payment was in the form of jewels,

Right: Parure of emerald and diamond jewellery made from emeralds given to Lord Harris following his victory over Tipu Sultan. Made in the mid- or late nineteenth century.

Far right: Art Deco bracelet of emeralds, rubies and diamonds, with the empty nineteenth-century ring mount that probably provided some of the stones for the bracelet.

taken from Tipu Sultan's legendary treasury at Seringapatam. Although the family sold most of them soon after, we know that Mrs Harris kept one emerald necklace and one ruby necklace with three emerald drops, and that these were re-made and worn by successive generations. In their current form, the ruby necklace, brooch and bracelet date from the late nineteenth century when they were re-set for Lucy Ada, who married the 4th Lord Harris in 1874. The ruby earrings and ring are much later, made at some point between 1920 and 1950. The

three emerald drops on the original Indian ruby necklace are probably those on the earrings and brooch of the more unified suite of emerald jewellery. It is possible that this parure was also made for Lucy Ada as she wears it with her coronation robes in a portrait of 1902. Alternatively it may have been made for Sarah, wife of the 3rd Lord Harris, who was married in 1850. A case for all the Harris jewels was made by Hancock's, and they travelled the Empire to support his role as a colonial administrator and international cricketer.

JEWELLERY BOXES

dominated by lavish silver toilet services with matching mirror, pincushion, cosmetic cases and caskets – which, despite not usually being lockable, were probably sometimes used for jewellery.

Queen Charlotte kept her magnificent jewellery (see page 60) in a specially designed inlaid-mahogany jewel cabinet made by London cabinetmakers Vile & Cobb, which stood in her bedroom in St James's Palace. However, after the end of the Season each year the grandest pieces were removed to the security of the Bank of England for safekeeping between July and January.

Some pieces of eighteenth- and nineteenth-century jewellery survive with their original velvet-lined cases of

Left: An informal portrait of Elizabeth Vernon, Countess of Southampton, by an unknown artist, c.1600. Her jewellery box, which echoes the design of a Tudor timber-framed house, has internal compartments lined with green fabric. Around it lie her jewels and a large pincushion with pins for fastening her clothing and attaching her

jewellery. The two necklaces at the end of her dressing table fasten with red-ribbon ties.

Below: Jewel casket of iron, made in Germany in the sixteenth century (length 29.8cm/11.7in). Open, it reveals the elaborate lock mechanism of the lid and five compartments lined with stamped velvet.

Jewellery boxes have a triple role of protecting delicate pieces of jewellery from damage and valuable pieces from theft and, if possible, of being decorative as well. Different balances of security and decorativeness have always been feasible, depending on individual requirements and wealth.

Small iron or steel caskets, resembling miniature coffers, were used throughout Europe for jewellery and valuables from the Middle Ages until around 1700. The steel was often decoratively pierced, and the iron might be covered with velvet or painted. Although usually subdivided into small compartments, these were for general use and not specifically designed to cradle individual pieces. They may sometimes be seen in contemporary paintings and tapestries, perhaps open on a dressing table. By the late seventeenth century the grandest dressing tables were

stamped and gilded leather. These were individually made to fit around the jewellery like a glove – consequently they are sometimes rather odd in shape. Fastened only with a simple clasp, they give protection but not security and rely on being kept in a safe or strong room. Custom-made boxes continued to be made and supplied with new pieces, usually with a more regular exterior profile and with specially cut, padded hollows and channels inside, which give full support to the jewel. They are often simply but elegantly decorated, and by the nineteenth century most are stamped inside with the jeweller's name and address. In Trollope's *The Eustace Diamonds* the family's valuable necklace had its own morocco leather case, but for safety was kept with their London jeweller when it was not being worn. Much to the alarm of all who knew its value, Lizzie – the young widow determined to keep the necklace for herself – had made for it an iron 'strong box, which was so heavy that she could barely lift it herself', which she kept in her bedroom.

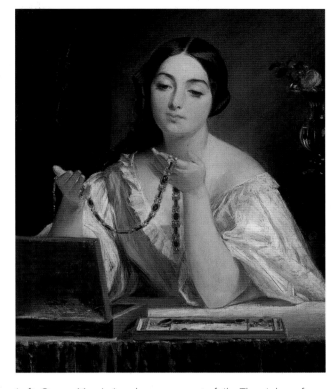

Left: Queen Mary's Jewel Casket, made towards the end of the seventeenth century, probably by the Bickford family, who were royal locksmiths (height 24.5cm/9.6in). Of steel, covered with crimson velvet and overlaid with gilt-brass studs and blued-steel quatrefoils. The cipher of William and Mary adorns the keyholes, and it is by tradition believed to have been made to hold Queen Mary's dowry when she married William III.

Above: *The Toilette* by C. R. Leslie. In this Victorian painting a young woman pauses while dressing to admire the long necklace that she has just lifted from her jewellery box. The shallow box, with its removable tray, would have been made specifically to fit this set of jewellery and supplied by the jeweller when the pieces were bought.

RELINQUISHING WORLDLY VANITIES

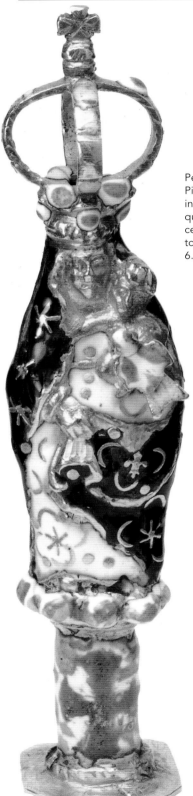

Pendant of the Virgin of the Pillar, enamelled gold, made in Saragossa in the second quarter of the seventeenth century as a pilgrim's offering to the shrine (height 6.4cm/2.5in).

Vanitas paintings, in which jewellery often features prominently, illustrate the transience of life and the folly of putting one's faith in this world's splendours. Similarly jewellery, one of the most enduring and precious of all worldly luxuries, has often inspired a contradictory impulse of renunciation. Over the centuries many men and women have hoped to either ease their path to salvation or salve their social consciences by the giving up of beautiful and valuable pieces of jewellery.

In the Middle Ages it was accepted practice to give or bequeath jewellery to a saint's shrine. Walter Reynolds, Archbishop of Canterbury, who died in 1327, left to the shrine of St Thomas à Becket both his pontifical ring with emeralds surrounding a magnificent sapphire that had once belonged to St Wulfstan and a second ring set with an engraved sapphire. He requested that they 'be fixed to the shrine of the glorious martyr aforesaid between the other jewels which I bought and gave over to the same shrine in times gone by'. Much later, in 1504, Ann Barrett left 'my corall bedys of thrys fifty, and my marrying ring', to the shrine of Our Lady of Walsingham. In England this custom was swept away by the Reformation, and these wealthy medieval treasuries were subsumed into the Royal jewel house.

However, the tradition has continued in many Catholic countries. In the mid-nineteenth century one of the very few Spanish shrines to have escaped secularization or being plundered by Napoleon's army, that of the Virgin of the Pillar at Saragossa, could boast a stunning collection of secular jewels from the sixteenth, seventeenth and early eighteenth centuries. This Spanish cult is derived from the story that in AD 40, the Virgin Mary was miraculously transported from Palestine to the banks of the river Ebro. Before returning to Palestine she asked for a church to be built around the marble pillar on which she stood, and this church became a great centre of pilgrimage. In 1870 they chose to auction many of the jewelled offerings to finance the building of a larger church, and the V&A took the opportunity to acquire a range of pieces, spending a little over £880 (see pages 51, 53 and 58).

The spirit of renunciation has persisted, albeit usually with the more secular emphasis of public benefaction. In the 1890s one of the finest collections of jewellery in America, valued at $2 million, was given by Mrs Leland Stanford, the wife of a railroad millionaire, to Stanford University to raise money for the library. Her generosity is commemorated on library bookplates that show her offering up her casket of jewels to Minerva, the goddess of wisdom. More recently there have been many high-profile auctions where the proceeds have gone to charitable causes, notably the sale of the Duchess of Windsor's jewellery in 1987, which benefited medical research.

Above: Detail of the central section set with assorted ring bezels encircled by a triple-strand pearl necklace. The jewellery is mostly nineteenth century in date.

Left: Flemish monstrance of silver and silver-gilt: the foot c.1650 and the upper section c.1530. It has been studded and hung with later votive offerings of jewellery.

APPENDIX OF ILLUSTRATIONS

Endpapers
Front: *La Jouaillier*. Photograph courtesy of the Bibliothèque Nationale, Paris.

Frontispiece
Lady Cory with Dog. Private Collection.

MATERIALS

Gold
Etruscan rosette. V&A: 8839-1863. Location: Jewellery Gallery 10.A.1.
The Shannongrove Gorget. V&A: M.35-1948. Given by Colonel C. K. Howard Bury. Location: Jewellery Gallery 39.E.3.
Coloured golds. Lid of Swiss box. V&A: 172-1878. Bequeathed by George Mitchell. Location: Jewellery Gallery 4.E.32.
Gold bars from South America. Photograph courtesy of Christies' Images Ltd. 1999.

Silver and Platinum
'Oxidized' silver bracelet by Rudolphi. V&A: M.50-1981. Location: Jewellery Gallery 20.E.15.
Diamond bow brooch, detail of back. V&A: M.93-1951. Bequeathed by Lady Jane Cory. Location: Jewellery Gallery 16.B.2.
Silver filigree brooch. V&A: 84-1872. Location: Room 102.
Diamonds and onyx set in platinum. V&A: M.212-1976. Given by Lady Reigate. Location: Jewellery Gallery 22.B.

Base Metals
Cut-steel button and blued-steel buckle. V&A: Circ.9-1936. Anonymous gift. V&A: 944-1864. Given by the Revd R. Brooke. Location: Room 114.
Aluminium and gilt-metal bracelet. V&A: M.24-1983.
Marcasite and blue-glass necklace. V&A: M.164-1975. Given by Dame Joan Evans. Location: Jewellery Gallery 17.C.2.
Ring of tin inlaid with gold by Fritz Maierhofer. V&A: M.960-1983. Location: Jewellery Gallery 29.B.
Niobium earrings by Alan Craxford. V&A: M.13&a-1985. Location: Jewellery Gallery 30.B.

Diamonds
Coloured diamonds set as rings. V&A: 1172/9-1869. Bequeathed by the Revd Chauncey Hare Townshend. Location: Jewellery Gallery 31.B.1-8
Design for a pendant by Arnold Lulls. V&A: D.6-1896.
Diamond-grading box. Photograph courtesy of De Beers.
Different cuts. Diagram courtesy of De Beers.

Coloured Gemstones: The Townshend Collection
Rings set with coloured stones. V&A: (row 1) 1284/ 1254/ 1239/ 1277/ 1312/ 1257-1869; (row 2) 1317/ 1182/ 1190/ 1289/ 1302/ 1304-1869; (row 3) 1321/ 1280/ 1281-1869, M.7-1913, 1316/ 1309-1869; (row 4) 1271-1869, M.5-1913, 1318/ 1223-1869, M.108-1913, M.5-1913; (row 5) 1332/ 1243/ 1250/ 1294/ 1292-1869; (row 6) 1199/ 1261/ 1334/ 1324/ 1204/ 1205-1869; (row 7) 1209/ 1214/ 1825/ 1207/ 1829-1869. Most bequeathed by the Revd Chauncey Hare Townshend, and two by Sir A. H. Church. Location: Jewellery Gallery 31.A/B/C/D/E.

Pearls
Detail of cultured-pearl necklace. V&A: M.129-1987. Hole Bequest. Location: Jewellery Gallery 22.B.
The Canning Jewel. V&A: M.2697-1931. Given by Mrs Edward S. Harkness. Location: Jewellery Gallery 26.10.
Seed-pearl necklace. V&A: M.147-1984. Location: Jewellery Gallery 19.E.
Opening oyster shells. *From Pearls and Pearling Life* by Edwin Streeter

Other Organic Materials
Piqué stars. V&A: M.55&a-1916. Given by Arthur Myers Smith. Location: Jewellery Gallery 19.K.
Detail of coral tiara. V&A: Circ.382-1960. Location: Jewellery Gallery 20.C.4.
Miniature ivory carving in ring. V&A: 21-1883. Bequeathed by F. W. Daniels. Location: Jewellery Gallery 34.I.14.
Bog-oak brooch. V&A: Circ.365-1963. Given by Mrs Hull Grundy.
Hair bracelet with cameo clasp. V&A: M.64-1951. Bequeathed by Lady Jane Cory. Location: Jewellery Gallery 17.E.11.
Egg-shell brooch by Thomas Gentille. V&A: M.2-1988. Location: Jewellery Gallery 30.C.
Celluloid buckle. V&A: M.210&a-1977, given by Mrs M. Spenik. Location: Room 102.

Glass and Enamel
Ring set with imitation diamonds. V&A: M.20-1929. Location: Jewellery Gallery 33.L.18.
Émail en resille on brown glass pendant. V&A: 490-1897. Location: Jewellery Gallery 14.C.4.
Pâte-de-verre pendant by Gabriel Argy-Rousseau. V&A: Circ.206-1972. Location: Room 74.
Detail of circlet by Elsa Freund. V&A: M.12-1992. Given by Mrs Jane Hershey. Location: Jewellery Gallery 44.

CHRONOLOGY OF STYLE

Masterpieces of the Middle Ages
The Langdale Rosary. V&A: M30-1934. Location: Jewellery Gallery 12.D.7.
Jewelled ring brooch. V&A: 547-1897. Location: Jewellery Gallery 12.B.3.
Heart-shaped brooch. V&A: 86-1899. Location: Jewellery Gallery 12.B.20.
William Wytlesey's ring. V&A: M.191-1975. Given by Dame Joan Evans. Location: Jewellery Gallery 32.K.11.

Enamelled case. V&A: 218-1874. Location: Room 43.

The Renaissance Pendant
The Danny Jewel. V&A: M.97-1917. Location: Jewellery Gallery 12.I.9.
Gem-set prophylactic pendant. V&A: M.242-1975. Given by Dame Joan Evans. Location: Jewellery Gallery 12.I.1.
Rock crystal ship. V&A: 295-1854. Location: Jewellery Gallery 28.8.
Salamander. V&A: M.537-1910. Salting Bequest. Location: Jewellery Gallery 26.5.
Cupid. V&A: M.387-1911. Location: Jewellery Gallery 13.B.1.

Echoes of Antiquity
The Gatacre Jewel. V&A: M.7-1982. Location: Jewellery Gallery 26.9.
Portrait of Sir Christopher Hatton. By courtesy of the National Portrait Gallery, London. V&A: 630-1884. Location: Jewellery Gallery 12.I.3.
Ring with Medusa cameo. V&A: M.555-1910. Salting Bequest. Location: Jewellery Gallery 33.L.2.

Statements of Faith
The Tor Abbey Jewel. V&A: 3581-1856. Location: Jewellery Gallery 12.I.4.
IHS pendant. V&A: M.248-1923 Location: Jewellery Gallery 13.D.11.
Pelican in its piety. V&A: 335-1870. From the Treasury of the Cathedral of the Virgin of the Pillar, Saragossa. Location: Jewellery Gallery 26.11.
Verre églomisé pendant. V&A: 409-1873. From the Treasury of the Cathedral of the Virgin of the Pillar, Saragossa. Location: Jewellery Gallery 28.7.

Gloriana
The Heneage Jewel. V&A: M.81-1935. Given by Lord Wakenfield through the National Art Collections Fund. Location: Jewellery Gallery 13.D.2.
The Barbor Jewel. V&A: 889-1894. Given by Miss M. Blencowe. Location: Jewellery Gallery 13.D.4.
Ruby-set miniature case. V&A: 4404-1857.
The Drake Jewel. Loan, private collection. Location: Jewellery Gallery 13.D

Necklaces of the Late Renaissance
Chain from the imperial castle of Ambras. V&A: 696-1868. Location: Jewellery Gallery 13.G.2.
Ruby-set chain. V&A: 35-1894. Location: Jewellery Gallery 13.G.9.
Chains from the Cheapside Hoard. V&A: M.1140-1926 and Loan, Museum of London. Location: Jewellery Gallery 13.C.

Tokens of Love
Renaissance heart brooch. V&A: M.461-1936. Given by Countess Harley Teleki. Location: Jewellery Gallery 13.I.1.

Marriage gimmel ring. V&A: M.224-1975.
Given by Dame Joan Evans. Location:
Jewellery Gallery 34.C.25.
Silver locket. V&A: M.3-1958. Bequeathed by
Mr S. H. J. Johnson. Location: Jewellery
Gallery 14.H.2.
Cupid slide. V&A: M.125-1962. Given by
Dame Joan Evans. Location: Jewellery
Gallery 27.B.9.

Bodice Ornaments of the Seventeenth Century
Bodice ornament, c.1630. V&A: M.143-1975.
Given by Dame Joan Evans. Location:
Jewellery Gallery 13.I.2.
Topaz bodice ornament and earrings. V&A:
M.98-b-1975. Given by Dame Joan Evans.
Location: Jewellery Gallery 14.G.4.

Stuart Jewellery
James I locket. V&A: M.92-1975. Given by
Dame Joan Evans. Location: Jewellery
Gallery 13.D.5.
Portrait of Anne of Denmark. Courtesy of the
National Portrait Gallery, London.
Charles I and II slide pendant. V&A: M.253-
1975. Given by Dame Joan Evans. Location:
Jewellery Gallery 14.H.3.
Charles II Boscobel Oak locket. V&A: 898-
1904. Location: Jewellery Gallery 14.H.16.

Riches from the New World
Dragon pendant. V&A: M.536-1910. Salting
Bequest. Location: Jewellery Gallery 26.8.
Order of the Inquisition. V&A: M.308-1910.
Location: Jewellery Gallery 14.G.6.
Emerald-set pendant. V&A: M.138-1975.
Given by Dame Joan Evans. Location:
Jewellery Gallery 14.G.1.
Emerald and diamond bodice ornament. V&A:
325-1870. From the Treasury of the
Cathedral of the Virgin of the Pillar,
Saragossa. Location: Jewellery Gallery 14.I.2.

Bows and True Lovers' Knots, 1650–1700
Necklace. V&A: M.95-1909. Bequeathed by
Lady Alma Tadema. Location: Jewellery
Gallery 14.A.5.
Fragment of chain. V&A: 4228-1857. Location:
Jewellery Gallery 14.B.14.
Small bow pin. V&A: 2824-1856. Location:
Jewellery Gallery 14.F.8.
Locket. V&A: 326-1870. From the Treasury of
the Cathedral of the Virgin of the Pillar,
Saragossa. Location: Jewellery Gallery 14.A.4.

Eighteenth-century Paste
Stomacher. V&A: M.134-1975. Given by Dame
Joan Evans. Location: Jewellery Gallery
15.A.1.
Opal paste necklace, earring, brooch and
buttons. V&A: M.159-1975, M.154a&b-1975,
M.157-1975 and M.154l&m-1975. Given by
Dame Joan Evans. Location: Jewellery
Gallery 16.A.
Paste dress clip. V&A: M.2-1989. Given by
Mrs Pamela Clabburn. Location: Jewellery
Gallery 16.C.

**Fashion Accessories: Shoe Buckles and
Châtelaines**
Pair of diamond and sapphire shoe buckles.
V&A: M.48&a-1962. Given by Dame Joan
Evans. Location: Jewellery Gallery 16.B.8.
Mourning shoe buckle. V&A: M.8-1973.
Location: Jewellery Gallery 15.F.1.
Silver and paste shoe buckle. V&A: 903-1900.
Location: Jewellery Gallery 15.F.8.
Silver and paste shoe buckle. V&A: M.40-1909.
Location: Jewellery Gallery 15.F.15.
Marcasite shoe buckle. V&A: M.51-1969.
Pfungst Reavil Bequest. Location: Jewellery
Gallery 15.F.14.
Gold châtelaine with watchcase. Loan, Barclays
Bank. Location: Jewellery Gallery 7.E.

Jewelled Bouquets
Enamelled bouquet. V&A: 319-1870. From the
Treasury of the Cathedral of the Virgin of the
Pillar, Saragossa. Location: Jewellery Gallery
15.D.3.
Flower spray. V&A: M.85-1951. Bequeathed by
Lady Jane Cory. Location: Jewellery Gallery
15.D.1.
Three *giardinetti* rings. V&A: 970-1871, 8550-
1863, M.50-1969. Pfungst Reavil Bequest.
Location: Jewellery Gallery 34.B.26/28/29.
Design for bouquet from the *Traité des pierres
précieuses*, Paris 1762.

Diamonds and Court Dress
Queen Charlotte by Allan Ramsay. Photograph
courtesy of Schloss Wilhelmshöhe, Cassel.
Set of three diamond bows. V&A: M.93/94&a-
1951. Bequeathed by Lady Jane Cory.
Location: Jewellery Gallery 16.B.2/3/4.
Diamond dress ornaments. V&A: M.95-1951.
Bequeathed by Lady Jane Cory. Location:
Jewellery Gallery 16.B.1.
Pair of bracelet clasps. V&A: M.51&a-1962.
Given by Dame Joan Evans. Location:
Jewellery Gallery 16.B.6.

Men's Jewellery
Masonic ring. V&A: 212-1870. Location:
Jewellery Gallery 34.B.1.
Pair of shoe buckles. V&A: M.9&a-1973.
Location: Jewellery Gallery 15.F.16.
Pair of knee buckles. V&A: 949&a-1864.
Given by the Revd R. Brooke. Location:
Jewellery Gallery 15.F.B.6.
Fob seal with intaglio of Trafalgar. V&A:
M.105-1945. Bequeathed by Miss P. M.
Sheward. Location: Jewellery Gallery 2.K.74.

Cut Steel
Cut-steel and jasperware button. V&A: M.4-
1969. Pfungst Reavil Bequest. Location:
Jewellery Gallery 17.D.4.
Cut-steel parure. V&A: M.306-1919. Joicey
Bequest. Location: Room 114.
Châtelaine. V&A: M.32-1969. Pfungst Reavil
Bequest. Location: Jewellery Gallery 18.F.
Cut-steel cartoon. Photograph courtesy of the
British Museum.

Sentimental Jewellery: For Love and Mourning
Trophy of love. V&A: M.37-1962. Given by
Dame Joan Evans. Location: Jewellery
Gallery 18.A.2.
Three mourning rings. V&A: 907-1888, M.162-
1962. Given by Dame Joan Evans. V&A: 915-
1888. Location: Jewellery Gallery 34.G.4/5
and 34.H.7.
Princess Charlotte mourning pendant. V&A:
M.82-1969. Given by Dame Joan Evans.
Location: Jewellery Gallery 27.A.14.
REGARD locket. V&A: M6-1986. Given by
Gerald Harris. Location: Jewellery Gallery
19.D.

Napoleon and Josephine
Cameo parure. Loan, private collection.
Location: Jewellery Gallery 17.F.3.
Emerald necklace and earrings. V&A: M.3-
1979. Given by Countess Margharita
Tagliavia. Location: Jewellery Gallery 17.F.2.
Josephine Spray. Loan, private collection.
Location: Jewellery Gallery 17.F.1.

Berlin Iron
Necklace. V&A: 96-1906. Location: Jewellery
Gallery 18.D.4.
Comb. V&A: 546-1899. Given by Sydney
Vacher. Location: Jewellery Gallery 18.D.3.
Earrings. V&A: 922&a-1852. Location:
Jewellery Gallery 18.D.12.

Souvenirs of the Grand Tour
Pietra-dura necklace. V&A: M.176-1941. Given
by Sir George R Lowndes. Location:
Jewellery Gallery 18.C.3.
Micromosaic brooch. V&A: M.35-1962. Given
by Dame Joan Evans. Location: Jewellery
Gallery 17.E.6.
Cameo brooch. V&A: M.274-1921. Given by
Mrs L. M. Festing. Location: Jewellery
Gallery 19.F.2.
Swiss enamel necklace. V&A: M.22-1985.
Location: Jewellery Gallery 19.J.

Jewellery of the 1820s and 1830s
Turquoise and pearl bow brooch. V&A: M.77-
1951. Bequeathed by Lady Jane Cory.
Location: Jewellery Gallery 19.A.1.
Pearl-grapes necklace. V&A: M.133-1951.
Bequeathed by Lady Jane Cory. Location:
Jewellery Gallery 19.F.5.
Brooch and earrings. V&A: M.265-b-1919.
Joicey Bequest. Location: Jewellery Gallery
19.F.7.
Portrait of Lady Stuart de Rothesay.
Photograph courtesy of the Government Art
Collection.

Mid-century Naturalism
Diamond bodice ornament. V&A: M.115-1951.
Bequeathed by Lady Jane Cory. Location:
Jewellery Gallery 19.I.3.
Turquoise and pearl convolvulus brooch. V&A:
M.82-1951. Bequeathed by Lady Jane Cory.
Location: Jewellery Gallery 20.B.9.

Amethyst-grapes necklace. V&A: M.135-1951.
Bequeathed by Lady Jane Cory. Location:
Jewellery Gallery 19.J.9.

The Great Exhibition, 1851
Bracelet by Froment-Meurice. V&A: 167-1854.
Location: Jewellery Gallery 20.D.10.
Part of parure by Pugin. V&A: M.10-1962,
M.20&21-1962. Given by Miss C. E.
Gladstone. Location: Jewellery Gallery
20.D.1/6/7.
Brooch with *commesso* of Queen Victoria.
V&A: M.340-1977. Location: Jewellery
Gallery 20.D.2.
Copy of the Royal Tara brooch. V&A: 920-
1852. Location: Jewellery Gallery 20.K.4.

The Archaeological Style
Necklace by Castellani. V&A: 638-1884.
Purchased from the sale of Alessandro
Castellani's effects. Location: Jewellery
Gallery 20.G.5.
Necklace by Giuliano. V&A: 163-1900.
Purchased from Giuliano. Location:
Jewellery Gallery 20.H.3.
Bracelet by Brogden. V&A: 735-1890. Bolckow
Bequest. Location: Jewellery Gallery 20.J.2.
Bracelet by Fabergé. V&A: M.170-1976. Given
by the National Art Collections Fund.
Location: Jewellery Gallery 20.J.13.
Scarab ring. V&A: M.40-1980. Location:
Jewellery Gallery 34.J.24.

The Renaissance Revival
Coral pendant by Froment-Meurice. V&A:
M.30-1962. Given by Dame Joan Evans.
Location: Jewellery Gallery 20.C.6.
Austrian necklace. V&A: 2664-1856. Location:
Jewellery Gallery 20.F.4.
Cameo-set pendant by Giuliano. V&A: 165-
1900. Given by C&A Giuliano. Location:
Jewellery Gallery 20.I.3.
Portrait of Elizabeth, Lady Seaton, by Edward
Long. Photograph courtesy of Plymouth City
Museums and Art Gallery collection.
Mermaid pendant by Wièse. V&A: M.15-1996.
Bequeathed by Deidre Inches Carr. Location:
Jewellery Gallery 20.I.

The Influence of Japan and India
Necklace by Falize. V&A: 1043-1871.
Purchased from Falize. Location: Jewellery
Gallery 21.C.2.
Japanese pouch fittings set as bracelet. V&A:
M.131-1984. Given by Mrs B. de B. Crichton.
Location: Jewellery Gallery 21.C.9.
Indian-style necklace by Phillips. V&A: 549-
1868. Purchased from Phillips. Location:
Jewellery Gallery 21.C.4.

The Locket
Locketomania cartoon by Alfred Thompson,
from *London Society* 1870 p.513.
Gold locket. V&A: M.11-1972. Given by Mrs
O. C. Leveson-Gower. Location: Jewellery
Gallery 21.B.16.

Locket bracelet. V&A: M.104-1951.
Bequeathed by Lady Jane Cory. Location:
Jewellery Gallery 21.B.3.
Bragg's component parts for handmade locket.
V&A: 913-1875. Purchased from Bragg.
Locket by Falize. V&A: 1045-1871. Purchased
from Falize. Location: Jewellery Gallery
21.C.6.

Novelties
'Blue creeper' earrings. V&A: AP.258-1875.
Beetle-set earrings. V&A: Circ.279&a-1960.
Given by Mrs Hull Grundy. Location: Room
102.
Skull stick pin. V&A: M.121-1984. Location:
Jewellery Gallery 20.E.
Engraving of mouse jewellery. From the *Queen*,
magazine, 31 July 1880.
Reverse-intaglio crystal of terrier. V&A: M.65-
1951. Bequeathed by Lady Jane Cory.
Location: Jewellery Gallery 20.K.7.

Nineteenth-century Machine-made Jewellery
Bragg's models and dies for brooch. V&A: 915-
1875. Purchased from Bragg. Engraving of
machinery from Streeter's catalogue of 1867.

Jet and Victorian Mourning
Jet parure. V&A: M.944-d-1983. Location:
Jewellery Gallery 20.L.
Portrait photograph of Elizabeth Howard.
Private collection.
Vulcanite cross. V&A: M.17-1971. Given by
Miss A. L. Wyatt. Location: Jewellery Gallery
20.L.2.

Art Nouveau from Paris and Brussels
Hornet brooch by Fouquet. V&A: 957-1901,
purchased from Fouquet at the Paris Salon,
1901. Location: Jewellery Gallery 21.H.1.
Orchid by Wolfers. V&A: M.11-1962.
Location: Jewellery Gallery 21H.6.
Wisteria dog collar. V&A: M.27-1962. Given
by Dame Joan Evans. Location: Jewellery
Gallery 21H.3.
Mistletoe brooch by Fouquet. V&A: M.19-
1979. Location: Jewellery Gallery 21.H.5.

The Jewellery of René Lalique, 1860–1945
Sweet-pea demi-parure. V&A: M.116-1966.
Location: Jewellery Gallery 21H.2.
Insects glass brooch. V&A: Circ.355-1971.
Location: Room 102.
Design for pendant. V&A: E.836-1949.

C. R. Ashbee and the Guild of Handicraft
Advertisement from the *British Architect*,
December 1903.
Enamelled-copper brooch. V&A: M.43-1980.
Location: Jewellery Gallery 22.A.3.
Peacock pendant with chain necklace. V&A:
M.23-1965. Location: Jewellery Gallery
21.F.3.
Ship pendant. V&A: M.4-1964. Bequeathed by
Miss M. C. Annesley. Location: Jewellery
Gallery 21.F.5.

The Art of Enamelling, *circa* 1900
The Wagner Girdle by Alexander Fisher. V&A:
M.20-1943. Given by Mrs O.E. Bostock and
Mr Ivan Horniman. Location: Jewellery
Gallery 21.E.4.
Cupid the Earth Upholder by Phoebe Traquair.
V&A: Circ.210-1953. Location: Jewellery
Gallery 21.F.8.
Tradescantia pendant by Nelson and Edith
Dawson. V&A: Circ.263-1955. Given by Mrs
Bickerdike and Miss M. Dawson. Location:
Jewellery Gallery 21.G.11.

May Morris's Jewellery
Ring by Charles Ricketts. V&A: M.35-1939.
Bequeathed by May Morris. Location:
Jewellery Gallery 34.K.9.
Jewellery designed by May Morris. V&A: M.17,
20, 21,24-1939. Given by Miss F. M. Vivian
Lobb. Location: Jewellery Gallery
21.D.19/14/6/20.
Jewellery inherited from Janey Morris. V&A:
M.37&a, 43, 39,40-1939. Bequeathed by May
Morris. Location: Jewellery Gallery
21.D.4/8/5/10.
Comb by Josef Hodel. V&A: M.18-1939.
Given by Miss F. M. Vivian Lobb. Location:
Jewellery Gallery 21.D.16.

Liberty's Cymric Jewellery
Waist clasp by Oliver Baker. V&A: M.306-
1975. Location: Jewellery Gallery 21.E.1.
Necklace by Archibald Knox. V&A: Circ.280-
1961. Location: Jewellery Gallery 21.G.1.
Buckle probably by Jessie M. King. V&A:
Circ.255-1964. Given by Mrs Hull Grundy.
Button. V&A: Circ.287-1961.

Henry Wilson and the Gaskins
Winged tiara by Henry Wilson. V&A:
Circ.362-1958. Given by the British Institute
of Industrial Arts. Location: Jewellery Gallery
21.I.2.
Pendant/cloak clasp by Henry Wilson. V&A:
M.13-1985. Location: Jewellery Gallery 21.I.
Design. V&A: E.669(498)-1955.
Enamelled necklace by the Gaskins. V&A:
Circ.359-1958. Given by Mrs Emmeline
Cadbury. Location: Jewellery Gallery 21.I.8.

Fashion Accessories, 1900–1930
Parasol handle by Gaillard. V&A: M.5-1980.
Location: Jewellery Gallery 21.J.10.
Silver cigarette box. V&A: T.111-1998. Given
by Mrs Herbert Seligmann.
Minaudière by Lacloche. V&A: M.24-1976.
Bequeathed by Miss J.H.G. Gollan. Location:
Jewellery Gallery 22.E.
Cigarette holder. V&A: Circ.40-1972. Location:
Jewellery Gallery 22.E.

Art Deco
Diamond and emerald necklace. V&A: M.139-
1987. Hole Bequest. Location: Jewellery
Gallery 22.D.

Clip by Cartier. V&A: M.36-1994. Bequeathed by Mr and Mrs Ernest Schwaiger. Location: Jewellery Gallery 22.D.
'Thunderbolt'. V&A: M.115-1993. Given by Josephine Elwes. Location: Jewellery Gallery 22.D.
Cypress tree brooch. V&A: M.25-1976. Bequeathed by Miss J. H. G. Gollan. Location: Jewellery Gallery 22.E.
Double clip. V&A: M.145-1987. Hole Bequest. Location: Jewellery Gallery 22.D.
Earrings by Janesich. V&A: M.24&a-1982. Location: Jewellery Gallery 22.B.
Long pendant/brooch. V&A: M.140-1987. Hole Bequest. Location: Jewellery Gallery 22.D.
Ring by Fouquet. V&A: M.4-1980. Location: Jewellery Gallery 34.K.15.
Brooch by Raymond Templier. V&A: M.18-1979. Location: Jewellery Gallery 22.D.

Two Profiles: Naum Slutzky and Alexander Calder
Bracelet by Naum Slutzky. V&A: Circ.1235-1967. Location: Jewellery Gallery 22.F.
Necklace by Naum Slutzky. V&A: Circ.1233-1967. Location: Jewellery Gallery 22.F.
Necklace by Alexander Calder. V&A: Circ.19-1962. Location: Jewellery Gallery 22.F.

The Post-war Decade, 1945–55
'Snake' necklace by Podolsky. V&A: M.29-1982. Location: Jewellery Gallery 23.A.
Brooch by Elisabeth Treskow. V&A: M.1-1988. Location: Jewellery Gallery 23.C.
Brooch by Henning Koppel for Jensen. V&A: Circ.136-1959. Location: Jewellery Gallery 23.C.
Buckle by Line Vautrin. V&A: M.33-1991. Location: Jewellery Gallery 22.F.

The International Exhibition of Modern Jewellery at Goldsmiths Hall, 1961
Necklace by E. R. Nele. V&A: Circ.475-1960.
Pendant by Elizabeth Frink. V&A: Circ.624-1962. Location: Jewellery Gallery 42.A.
Necklace by Terry Frost. V&A: Circ.620-1962. Location: Jewellery Gallery 42.A.
Brooch by Jean Arp. V&A: Circ.395-1962. Given by Johanan Peter. Location: Jewellery Gallery 42.A.
Ring by Alan Davie. V&A: Circ.376-1961. Location: Jewellery Gallery 34.K.19.

The 1960s
Brooch by John Donald. V&A: M.346-1977. Location: Jewellery Gallery 23.D.
Necklace by Gerda Flöckinger. V&A commission: Circ.319-1960. Location: Jewellery Gallery 23.D.
Brooch by Braque. V&A: M.5-1992. Location: Jewellery Gallery 23.D.
Ring by Jeanne Thé. Loan, private collection. Location: Jewellery Gallery 23.D.
Brooch by Louis Osman. V&A: M.40:2-1994. Given by Mrs Phillida Shaw and Mrs Linda Morley.

Neckpiece by Helga Zahn. V&A: M.7-1991. Given by Herr Klaus Zahn. Location: Jewellery Gallery 44.
Bracelet by Gijs Bakker. V&A: M.33-1990. Location: Jewellery Gallery 23.D.
Ring by Gerda Flöckinger. V&A: Circ.118-1971. Location: Jewellery Gallery 34.K.21.

The 1970s
Bracelet by Gerd Rothmann. V&A: M.30-1990. Location: Room 72.
Necklace by Wendy Ramshaw necklace. V&A: M.169-1976. Location: Jewellery Gallery 24.11.
Ring by Fritz Maierhofer. V&A: M.74-1988. Location: Jewellery Gallery 29.A.
Bracelet by Gerda Flöckinger. V&A: M.245-1977. Location: Jewellery Gallery 29.D.
Sycamore brooch by Malcolm Appleby. V&A: M.314-1977. Location: Jewellery Gallery 29.C.
Serpent bracelet by Courts & Hackett. V&A: M.285-1977. Location: Jewellery Gallery 29.C.
Neckpiece by David Watkins V&A: M.1-1978. Location: Jewellery Gallery 44.
Brooch by Edward de Large. V&A: M.2-1978. Location: Jewellery Gallery 42.B.

The 1980s
Cravat brooch by Arline Fisch.
Pendant by Vicky Ambery-Smith. V&A: M.40-1982. Location: Jewellery Gallery 30.A.
Necklace by Tone Vigeland. V&A: M.42-1984. Location: Jewellery Gallery 43.
Necklace by Robert Ebendorf. V&A: M.5-1989. Given by Tom Weisz. Location: Jewellery Gallery 30.D.
Necklace by Jacqueline Mina. V&A: M.1-1987. Commissioned jointly by the Platinum Shop, Ayreton Metals and the V&A. Location: Jewellery Gallery 24.
Fish-head brooch by Simon Costin. V&A commission: M.61-1988. Location: Room 72.
Bracelet by Friedrich Becker. V&A: M.23-1991. Location: Jewellery Gallery 43.
Brooch by William Harper. V&A: M.3-1990. Location: Jewellery Gallery 30.B.
Brooch by Kevin Coates. V&A: M.16-1996. Anonymous gift. Location: Jewellery Gallery 30.B.
Necklace by Charlotte de Syllas. V&A commission: M.4-1990. Location: Jewellery Gallery 30.A.
Brooch by Jamie Bennett. V&A: M.4-1996. Given by Sam Booton. Location: Jewellery Gallery 30.D.
Picasso's Ladies neckpiece by Wendy Ramshaw. V&A: M.29-1998.

The 1990s
Brooch by Yasuki Hiramatsu. V&A: M.1-1991. Location: Jewellery Gallery 30.D.
Bracelet by Giampaolo Babetto. V&A: M.48-1990. Location: Jewellery Gallery 30.D.
Boxed necklace set by Hermann Junger. V&A: M.24-1991. Location: Jewellery Gallery 43.

Brooch and ring by Elisabeth Holder. V&A: M.25-1991 and M.29-1992. Location: Jewellery Gallery 30.
Necklace by Breon O'Casey. V&A: M.1-1996. Given by Helen W. Drutt English. Location: Jewellery Gallery 44.
Earrings by Catherine Martin. V&A: M.20-1995. Location: Jewellery Gallery 43.
Brooch by Peter Chang. V&A: M.37-1992. Location: Jewellery Gallery 30.C.
'Mediterranean' bracelet by ROY. Promised gift to the V&A. Photograph by Dean Powell, courtesy of the artist.
Neckpiece by Marjorie Schick. V&A: M.58-1997.
Three necklaces by Cynthia Cousens. V&A commission: M.47, 48, 49-1996.

MANUFACTURING AND DISTRIBUTION

Hallmarking and Design Registration
Mourning ring. V&A: 653-1864. Given by the Rev. R. Brooke. Location: Jewellery Gallery 34.G.29.
'Scottish pebble' brooch. V&A: Circ.278-1961. Location: Jewellery Gallery 20.K.8.
Bracelet with detail of marks. V&A: M.23-1989. Given by Ruth C. Harris. Location: Jewellery Gallery 21.A.
Details of Fabergé bracelet marks. V&A: M.170-1976. Location: Jewellery Gallery 20.J.13.

Shops
Sixteenth-century engraving. Photograph courtesy of the Worshipful Goldsmiths Company.
Hawley's shop. Photograph courtesy of the British Museum.
Interior view of Fouquet's shop. V&A: PP 19 G *The Ladies Realm*, xv, 1903–4

Tracing a Jewel's History
The Harris Jewels. Private Collection. Location: Jewellery Gallery 35.A/B/C

Jewellery Boxes
Iron jewel casket. V&A: M.27-1911. Location: Room 114.
Mary II's jewel casket. V&A: M.19-1937.
The Toilette by C. R. Leslie. V&A: FA.125, Sheepshanks Gift, 1857.
Portrait of Elizabeth Vernon, Countess of Southampton by an unknown artist *c.* 1610. Photograph courtesy of His Grace, the Duke of Buccleuch, K.T., V.R.D., from his Collection at Boughton House, Northamptonshire, England.

Relinquishing Worldly Vanities
Virgin of the Pillar pendant. V&A: 343-1870. From the Treasury of the Cathedral of the Virgin of the Pillar, Saragossa. Location: Jewellery Gallery 13.E.8.
Flemish monstrance set with jewellery. Loan, private collection.

BIBLIOGRAPHY

PUBLICATIONS ON THE V&A'S COLLECTION

Bury, S. *Jewellery Gallery Summary Catalogue* Victoria & Albert Museum London 1982; out of print but available on microfiche through the Department of Metalwork, Silver and Jewellery at the V&A. An illustrated, full-colour microfiche is purchasable from: Emmett Publishing, Hindhead, Surrey GU26 6QN

Bury, S. *An Introduction to Rings* London 1984

Bury, S. *An Introduction to Sentimental Jewellery* London 1985

Campbell, M. *An Introduction to Medieval Enamels* London 1983

Lightbown, R. *Medieval European Jewellery* London 1992

Oman, C. *Catalogue of Rings* Victoria & Albert Museum London 1930; repr. Ipswich 1993

Somers Cocks, A. *An Introduction to Courtly Jewellery* London 1980

BIBLIOGRAPHY

Addison, K. J. & S. *Pearls: Ornament and Obsession* London 1992

Antwerp Diamond Museum *A Sparkling Age: 17th-century Diamond Jewellery* Antwerp 1993

Antwerp Koningin Fabiolalazaal *The Jewel: Sign and Symbol* Antwerp 1995

Baarsen, R., & Van Berge, G. *Jewellery, 1820–1920* Amsterdam 1990

Balfour, I. *Famous Diamonds* London 1997

Bard Graduate Center *Cast Iron from Central Europe, 1800–1850* New York 1994

Barten, S. *René Lalique: Schmuck und Objets d'art, 1890–1910* Munich 1977

Bayerisches Nationalmuseum *Müncher Schmuck, 1900–1940* Munich 1990

Becker, V. *Antique and 20th-century Jewellery* London 1980

Becker, V. *Art Nouveau Jewellery* London 1985

Becker, V. *The Jewellery of René Lalique* for the exhibition May–July 1987, Goldsmiths' Hall, London

Becker, V. *Fabulous Fakes* London 1988

Bennet, D., & Mascetti, D. *Understanding Jewellery* London 1989

Black, A. J. *A History of Jewels* London 1981

Blair, C. (ed.) *The Crown Jewels* London 1999

Boardman, J., & Scarisbrick, D. *The Ralph Harari Collection of Finger Rings* London 1977

Brunhammer, Y. (ed.) *The Jewels of Lalique* Paris 1998

Bury, S. *Jewellery, 1789–1910: The International Era* Woodbridge 1991

Campbell, M. 'Gold, Silver and Precious Stones', in *English Medieval Industries*, Blair, J. & Ramsay, N. (eds) London 1991

Cartlidge, B. *Twentieth-century Jewelry* New York 1985

Cavill, K., Cocks, G., & Grace, J. *Australian Jewellers, Gold and Silversmiths: Makers and Marks* Roseville, NSW 1992

Cera, D. F. (ed.) *Jewels of Fantasy: Costume Jewelry of the 20th Century* New York, 1992

Chadour, A. B. *Rings: The Alice and Louis Koch Collection: Forty Centuries Seen by Four Generations* Leeds 1994

Chadour, A. B., & Joppien, R. *Schmuck I & II*, Cologne 1985

Chanlot, A. *Les Ouvrages en Cheveux, Leurs Secrets* Paris 1986

Cherry, J. *Medieval Craftsmen: Goldsmiths* London 1992

Clifford, A. *Cut-steel and Berlin-iron Jewellery* Bath 1971

Crafts Council *Crafts Magazine*

Crafts Council *Shining Through* London 1995

Culme, J. *Directory of Gold and Silversmiths: Jewellers & Allied Trades, 1838–1914* Woodbridge 1987

Cumming, E. *Phoebe Anna Traquair, 1852–1936* Edinburgh 1993

Cummins, G., & Taunton, N. *Châtelaines. Utility to Glorious Extravagance* Woodbridge 1994

Dalgleish, G., & Marshall, R. *The Art of Jewellery in Scotland* Edinburgh 1991

Dalton, O. M. *Catalogue of the Finger Rings, Early Christian, Byzantine, Teutonic, Medieval and Later. Franks Bequest* London 1912

de Vasconcelos e Sousa, D. G. *Reais Joias no Norte de Portugal*, Porto 1995

Dietz, U., Joselit, J., Smead, K., & Zapata, J. *The Glitter and the Gold: Fashioning America's Jewelry* Newark, NJ 1997

D'Orey, L. *Five Centuries of Jewellery: National Museum of Ancient Art, Lisbon* London 1995

Dormer, P., & Turner, R. *The New Jewelry: Trends and Traditions* London 1985

Drutt English, H., & Dormer, P. *Jewelry of Our Time: Art, Ornament and Obsession* London 1995

Dubin, L. S. *History of Beads* New York 1987

Egger, G. *Bürgerlicher Schmuck* Munich 1984

Ettinger, R. *Popular Jewelry, 1840–1940* Pennsylvania 1990

Evans, J. *Magical Jewels of the Middle Ages and the Renaissance* Oxford 1922

Evans, J. *A History of Jewellery, 1100–1870* London 1970

Field, L. *The Jewels of Queen Elizabeth II: Her Personal Collection* London 1992

Flower, M. *Victorian Jewellery* London 1951, rev. 1967

Fraquet, H. *Amber* London 1987

Gabardi, M. *Gioielli Anni '50* Milan 1986

Gabardi, M. *Art Deco Jewellery, 1920–1949* Woodbridge 1989

Game, A., & Goring, A. *Jewellery Moves: Ornament for the 21st Century* Edinburgh 1998

Gandy Fales, M. *Jewelry in America* Woodbridge 1995

Gere, C. *Victorian Jewellery Design* London 1972

Gere, C. *European & American Jewellery, 1830–1914* London 1975

Gere, C., & Munn, G. C. *Artists' Jewellery Pre-Raphaelite to Arts and Crafts* Woodbridge 1989

Gorewa, O., Polynina, I., Rachmanov, N., & Raimann, A. *Joyaux du Trésor de Russie* Paris 1991

Grant Lewin, S. *One of a Kind: American Art Jewelry Today* New York 1994

Hackenbroch, Y. *Renaissance Jewellery* London 1979

Hackenbroch, Y. *Enseignes: Renaissance Hat Jewels* Florence 1996

Hase-Schmunt, U., Weber, C., & Becker, I. *Theodor Fahrner* Pennsylvania 1991

Hearn, K. *Dynasties: Painting in Tudor and Jacobean England, 1530–1630* London 1995

Hinks, P. *Nineteenth-century Jewellery* London 1975

Hinks, P. *Twentieth-century British Jewellery, 1900–1980* London 1983

Hinks, P. *Victorian Jewellery: A Complete Compendium of over Four Thousand Pieces of Jewellery* London 1991

Houston, J. *Caroline Broadhead. Jewellery in Studio* London 1990

Hughes, B. & T. *Georgian Shoe Buckles. Illustrated by the Lady Maufe Collection of Shoe Buckles at Kenwood* London 1972

Hughes, G. *Modern Jewelry: An International Survey, 1890–1963* London 1963

Johnson, P., & Garner, P. (eds) *Art Nouveau: The Anderson Collection* Sainsbury Centre for Visual Arts Norwich, undated

Jonas, S., & Nissenson, M. *Cuff Links* New York 1991

Joppien, R. *Elisabeth Treskow* Cologne 1990

Karlin, E. Z. *Jewelry & Metalwork in the Arts & Crafts Tradition* Philadelphia 1993

Koch, M. *et al. The Belle Époque of French Jewellery, 1850–1910* London 1991

Köchert, I. H. *Köchert Jewellery Designs, 1810–1940* Florence 1990

Landesmuseum *Schmuckkunst der moderne Grossbritannien* Mainz 1995

Lanllier, J., & Pini, M.-A. *Cinq Siècles de Joaillerie en Occident* Fribourg 1971

Lenti, L. *Gioielli e Gioiellieri di Valenza Arte e Storia Orafa, 1825–1975* Turin 1994

Lesley Craze Gallery *Today's Jewels: From Paper to Gold* London 1993

Lesley, P. *Renaissance Jewels and Jeweled Objects from the Melvin Gutman Collection* Baltimore 1968

Lewis, M. D. S. *Antique Paste Jewellery* London 1970

Luthi, A. L. *Sentimental Jewellery: Antique Jewels of Love and Sorrow* Princes Risborough 1998

Manhart, T. *William Harper: Artist as Alchemist* Orlando, Florida 1989

Marquardt, B. *Schmuck: Klassizismus und Biedermeier, 1780–1850: Deutschland, Österreich, Schweiz* Munich 1983

Marquardt, B. *Schmuck: Realismus und Historismus, 1850–1895: Deutschland, Österreich, Schweiz* Munich 1998

Martin, S. *Archibald Knox* London 1995

Mascetti, D., & Triossi, A. *Earrings from Antiquity to the Present* London 1990

Mascetti, D., & Triossi, A. *Bulgari* Milan 1996

Medvedeva, G. *et al. Russian Jewellery, 16th– 20th Centuries: From the Collection of the Historical Museum, Moscow* Moscow 1987

Menkes, S. *The Windsor Style* London 1987

Metropolitan Museum of Art *Treasures of Early Irish Art* New York 1977

Metropolitan Museum of Art *The Age of Napoleon* New York 1989

Metropolitan Museum of Art *Metropolitan Jewelry* New York 1991

Meyerowitz, P. *Jewelry and Sculpture through Unit Construction* London 1967

Morel, B. *The French Crown Jewels* Antwerp 1988

Mould, P. *The English Shoe Buckle* Wirral undated

Muller, H. *Jet* London 1987

Muller, P. *Jewels in Spain, 1500–1800* New York 1972

Mulvagh, J. *Costume Jewellery in Vogue* London 1988

Munn, G. C. *Castellani and Giuliano* London 1984

Munn, G. C. *The Triumph of Love: Jewelry, 1530–1930* London 1993

Musée des Arts Décoratifs *René Lalique: Bijoux, Verre* Paris 1991

Museum Bellerive *De Fouquet, 1860–1960: Schmuck Künstler in Paris* Zurich 1984

Museum of London *Dress Accessories: Medieval Finds from Excavations in London* London 1991

Museum of London *Treasures and Trinkets. Jewellery in London from Pre-Roman Times to the 1930s* London 1991

Museum voor Sierkunst *Japanese Contemporary Jewellery* Ghent 1995

Nadelhoffer, H. *Cartier* London 1984

Natural History Museum *Gemstones* London 1987

Naylor, G. *The Arts and Crafts Movement* London 1971

Néret, G. *Boucheron* New York 1988

Newman, H. *An Illustrated Dictionary of Jewelry* London 1981

Northampton Museum *Catalogue of Shoe and Other Buckles* Northampton 1981

O'Day, D. *Victorian Jewellery* London 1974

Ogden, J. *et al. Jewellery: Makers, Motifs, History, Techniques* London 1989

Oman, C. *British Rings, 800–1914* London 1974

Pforzheim Schmuckmuseum *Ornamenta 1* Munich 1989

Phillips, C. *Jewelry: From Antiquity to the Present* London 1986

Pointon, M. *Strategies for Showing: Women, Possession and Representation in English Visual Culture, 1665–1800* Oxford 1997

Proddow, P., & Healy, D. *American Jewelry: Glamour and Tradition* New York 1987

Proddow, P., Healy, D., & Fasel, M. *Hollywood Jewels* New York 1992

Pullée, C. *20th-century Jewelry* London 1990

Purcell, K. *Falize: A Dynasty of Jewellers* London 1999

Rainwater, D. T. *American Jewelry Manufacturers* Pennsylvania 1988

Ramshaw, W. (ed.) *Picasso's Ladies: Jewellery by Wendy Ramshaw* Stuttgart 1998

Ramshaw, W. *Jewel Drawings and Projects* Barcelona 1998

Raulet, S. *Art Deco Jewelry* London 1985

Rudoe, J. *Cartier, 1900–1939* London 1997

Rudolph, M. *Naum Slutzky: Meister am Bauhaus, Goldschmied und Designer* Germany 1990

Scarisbrick, D. *Ancestral Jewels* London 1989

Scarisbrick, D. *Rings: Symbols of Wealth, Power and Affection* London 1993

Scarisbrick, D. *Jewellery in Britain, 1066–1837* Norwich 1994

Scarisbrick, D. *Chaumet* Paris 1995

Scarisbrick, D. *Tudor and Jacobean Jewellery* London 1995

Schiffer, N. *The Power of Jewelry* Pennsylvania 1988

Schofield, A., & Fahy, K. *Australian Jewellery, 19th and Early 20th Century* Woodbridge 1991

Scottish Arts Council *Jewellery in Europe* 1975

Snowman, A. K. *The Art of Carl Fabergé* London 1953

Snowman, A. K. (ed.) *The Master Jewelers* London 1990

Society of Jewellery Historians *Jewellery Studies*

Solodkoff, A. *Russian Gold and Silver* London 1981

Somers Cocks, A. *An Introduction to Courtly Jewellery* London 1980

Somers Cocks, A., & Truman, C. *The Thyssen-Bornemisza Collection: Renaissance Jewels, Gold Boxes and Objets de Vertu* London 1995

Sotheby's *The Jewels of the Duchess of Windsor* Sale Catalogue, Geneva, April 1987

Streeter, Patrick *Streeter of Bond Street: A Victorian Jeweller* Harlow, Essex 1993

Taburet-Delahaye, E. *L'Orfèvrerie Gothique au Musée de Cluny, XIIIe–Début XVe Siècle* Paris 1989

Tait, H. (ed.) *Jewellery through 7000 Years* London 1976

Tait, H., Wilson, T., Rudoe, J., & Gere, C. *The Art of the Jeweller: A Catalogue of the Hull Grundy Gift to the British Museum* London 1984

Tait, H. *Catalogue of the Waddesdon Bequest in the British Museum: Volume I: The Jewels* London 1986

Taylor, G., & Scarisbrick, D. *Finger Rings from Ancient Egypt to the Present Day* Oxford 1978

Thage, J. *Danish Jewelry* Boger 1990

Tilbrook, A. J., & House, G. *The Designs of Archibald Knox for Liberty & Co.* London 1976

Tillander, H. *Diamond Cuts in Historic Jewellery, 1381–1910* London 1995

Triossi, A., & Mascetti, D. *The Necklace: From Antiquity to the Present* London 1997

Turner, R. *Contemporary Jewelry: A Critical Assessment, 1945–75* London 1976

Turner, R. *Jewelry in Europe: New Times, New Thinking* London 1996

Twining, E. F. *A History of the Crown Jewels of Europe* London 1960

Untracht, O. *Jewelry Concepts and Technology* London 1982

Valcke, J., & Dupont, P.-P. *Contemporary Belgian Jewellery* Liège 1992

Vautrin, L., & Mauriès, P. *Line Vautrin: Sculptor, Jeweller, Magician* London 1992

Vever, H. *La Bijouterie Française au XIXe Siècle* Paris 1908

Victoria & Albert Museum *Jewellery by Gerda Flöckinger/Glass by Sam Herman* London 1971

Victoria & Albert Museum *Liberty's, 1875–1975* London 1975

Victoria & Albert Museum/Debrett *Princely Magnificence: Court Jewels of the Renaissance, 1500–1630* London 1980

Victoria and Albert Museum *Wendy Ramshaw* London 1982

Victoria and Albert Museum *Modern Artists' Jewels* London 1984

Victoria and Albert Museum *Kevin Coates* London 1985

Victoria and Albert Museum *Alan Craxford* London 1985

Victoria and Albert Museum *Jacqueline Mina: Jewellery, 1973–1985* London 1985

Victoria and Albert Museum *Gerda Flöckinger* London 1986

Victoria and Albert Museum *Fritz Maierhofer* London 1988

von Hapsburg, G., & Lopato, M. *Fabergé: Imperial Jeweller* London 1994

von Hase, U. *Schmuck in Deutschland und Österreich, 1895–1914* Munich 1977

Walters Art Gallery *Jewelry: Ancient to Modern* Baltimore 1979

Ward, A., Cherry, J., Gere, C., & Cartlidge, B. *The Ring from Antiquity to the Twentieth Century* London 1981

Watkins, D. *The Best in Contemporary Jewellery* London 1993

Weber, C. *Schmuck: Der 20er und 30er Jahre in Deutschland* Stuttgart 1990

Whitehead, R. *Buckles, 1250–1800* Essex 1996

Worshipful Company of Goldsmiths *International Exhibition of Modern Jewellery, 1890–1961* Kent 1961

Youngs, S. (ed.) *The Work of Angels: Masterpieces of Celtic Metalwork, AD 6th–9th Centuries* London 1989

Zapata, J. *The Jewelry and Enamels of Louis Comfort Tiffany* New York 1993

Zucker, B. *Gems and Jewels* London 1984

INDEX

Lüstres

Les sbaieres d'or et d'Argent de
Veniise, de Dieppe d'Escaille
d'Yvoir, et plusieurs autres

Évantails en mignature et autres
Canes garnie d'Or et d'Argent

Pagottes de la Chines et autres
Monstres d'Or, et d'Argent,
et plusieurs Bijoux a la mode

N. de l'Armessin juven. et sculp.

La Jouaillier.

a Paris Chez N. de l'Armessin Rue S. Iaques pres la Rue du Platre a la Coupe d'or Aueq Priuileg. du Roy. 1695.